Between the World and the Urban Classroom

TRANSGRESSIONS: CULTURAL STUDIES AND EDUCATION

Cultural studies provides an analytical toolbox for both making sense of educational practice and extending the insights of educational professionals into their labors. In this context *Transgressions: Cultural Studies and Education* provides a collection of books in the domain that specify this assertion. Crafted for an audience of teachers, teacher educators, scholars and students of cultural studies and others interested in cultural studies and pedagogy, the series documents both the possibilities of and the controversies surrounding the intersection of cultural studies and education. The editors and the authors of this series do not assume that the interaction of cultural studies and education devalues other types of knowledge and analytical forms. Rather the intersection of these knowledge disciplines offers a rejuvenating, optimistic, and positive perspective on education and educational institutions. Some might describe its contribution as democratic, emancipatory, and transformative. The editors and authors maintain that cultural studies helps free educators from sterile, monolithic analyses that have for too long undermined efforts to think of educational practices by providing other words, new languages, and fresh metaphors. Operating in an interdisciplinary cosmos, *Transgressions: Cultural Studies and Education* is dedicated to exploring the ways cultural studies enhances the study and practice of education. With this in mind the series focuses in a non-exclusive way on popular culture as well as other dimensions of cultural studies including social theory, social justice and positionality, cultural dimensions of technological innovation, new media and media literacy, new forms of oppression emerging in an electronic hyperreality, and postcolonial global concerns. With these concerns in mind cultural studies scholars often argue that the realm of popular culture is the most powerful educational force in contemporary culture. Indeed, in the twenty-first century this pedagogical dynamic is sweeping through the entire world. Educators, they believe, must understand these emerging realities in order to gain an important voice in the pedagogical conversation.

Without an understanding of cultural pedagogy's (education that takes place outside of formal schooling) role in the shaping of individual identity – youth identity in particular – the role educators play in the lives of their students will continue to fade. Why do so many of our students feel that life is incomprehensible and devoid of meaning? What does it mean, teachers wonder, when young people are unable to describe their moods, their affective affiliation to the society around them. Meanings provided young people by mainstream institutions often do little to help them deal with their affective complexity, their difficulty negotiating the rift between meaning and affect. School knowledge and educational expectations seem as anachronistic as a ditto machine, not that learning ways of rational thought and making sense of the world are unimportant.

But school knowledge and educational expectations often have little to offer students about making sense of the way they feel, the way their affective lives are shaped. In no way do we argue that analysis of the production of youth in an electronic mediated world demands some "touchy-feely" educational superficiality. What is needed in this context is a rigorous analysis of the interrelationship between pedagogy, popular culture, meaning making, and youth subjectivity. In an era marked by youth depression, violence, and suicide such insights become extremely important, even life saving. Pessimism about the future is the common sense of many contemporary youth with its concomitant feeling that no one can make a difference.

If affective production can be shaped to reflect these perspectives, then it can be reshaped to lay the groundwork for optimism, passionate commitment, and transformative educational and political activity. In these ways cultural studies adds a dimension to the work of education unfilled by any other sub-discipline. This is what *Transgressions: Cultural Studies and Education* seeks to produce – literature on these issues that makes a difference. It seeks to publish studies that help those who work with young people, those individuals involved in the disciplines that study children and youth, and young people themselves improve their lives in these bizarre times.

Between the World and the Urban Classroom

Edited by

George Sirrakos Jr.
Kutztown University, Pennsylvania, USA

and

Christopher Emdin
Teachers College, Columbia University, New York, USA

SENSE PUBLISHERS
ROTTERDAM/BOSTON/TAIPEI

A C.I.P. record for this book is available from the Library of Congress.

ISBN: 978-94-6351-030-1 (paperback)
ISBN: 978-94-6351-031-8 (hardback)
ISBN: 978-94-6351-032-5 (e-book)

Published by: Sense Publishers,
P.O. Box 21858,
3001 AW Rotterdam,
The Netherlands
https://www.sensepublishers.com/

All chapters in this book have undergone peer review.

Cover design by Elham Ataeiazar

Printed on acid-free paper

To the memory of my mother,
Barbara 'Barbie' Sirrakos

– George Sirrakos Jr.

To Ebone, Sydney, and Malcolm.
Thank you for the inspiration.

– Christopher Emdin

TABLE OF CONTENTS

Foreword   xi
Bettina L. Love

Acknowledgments   xiii

Introduction   xv
George Sirrakos Jr. and Christopher Emdin

1. Media as Cultural Discourse and Youth Emancipation   1
   Arash Daneshzadeh

2. Necropolitics and Education   19
   Venus E. Evans-Winters

3. What the Resistance to High-Stakes Testing Can Teach Us about Urban
   Classrooms   35
   Wayne Au

4. Why You So Angry? Serena Williams, Black Girl Pain, and
   the Pernicious Power of Stereotypes   43
   Treva B. Lindsey

5. Beyond a Deficit Perspective: From the Greek Financial Crisis to
   Urban Students of Color   53
   George Sirrakos Jr.

6. Destroying the Spectacle in Urban Education: Embracing the New Danger   69
   Christopher Emdin

7. Beyond Beats, Rhymes, & Beyoncé: Hip Hop, Hip Hop Education,
   and Culturally Relevant Pedagogy   83
   Gloria Ladson-Billings

8. Sexuality Education and the School District of Philadelphia:
   The Importance of Community   95
   Patricia Walsh Coates

9. Ecocritical Urban Education: Responses to 21st Century Challenges   107
   Mark Wolfmeyer

Afterword: Onward Urban Soldiers   123
    Shirley R. Steinberg

About the Authors   125

FOREWORD

Sirrakos and Emdin sample the title of their book from Ta-Nehisi Coates's (2015), *Between the World and Me*. When I first read *Between the World and Me*, I was angry. Although Coates offers a sharp and brilliant critique of America's legacy of oppression and dispossession of Black people and how Black life is destroyed by "those Americans who believe that they are white" (p. 6), Coates's book ends without a whisper of hope. There was no "We shall overcome" or "We gon' be alright" moment.

When I got to the last few pages of Coates's book, I felt distraught and as if I had lost something that I knew I could never get back. I am too old and too critical of Whiteness, I thought, to be so uncomfortable by Coates's reading of our world. Yet, as an educator whose life's work centers on social justice, his words cut deep. Coates writes, "The fact of history is that black people have not—probably no people have ever—liberated themselves strictly through their own efforts" (p. 96). He goes on to write, speaking to his son, "The entire narrative of this country argues against the truth of who you are" (p. 99). With regard to education, Coates offered the following: "The streets were not my only problem. If the streets shackled my right leg, the schools shackled my left. Educated children never offered excuses— certainly not childhood itself. The world had no time for the childhoods of black boys and girls. How could the schools?" (p. 25).

What do you do with Coates's words? What do you do with feelings of hopelessness? Where does the fight begin when winning is bleak? *Between the World and the Urban Classroom* offers insights to the complex educational problems experienced by Coates and countless marginalized youth in urban schools. Sirrakos, Emdin, and the chapter contributors to the book provide what is indeed necessary: critical analyses of the pernicious combination of racism; economic, political, and racial isolation; sexism; poverty; mass incarceration; state sanctioned violence; racist testing practices; and necropolitics that Black and Brown youth face daily in urban classrooms. But this book also tells the story of the ways in which we resist and create pedagogies that will be tools in the fight for intersectional justice.

Youth of color are living and learning in school environments that are dead set on their destruction. Black and Brown youth are seen by our educational systems as disposable. Moreover, the structural systems of oppression offer no apologies for Black and Brown youth's disposability, and their cries of injustice are seen as excuses. I wish my words were hyperbole. I wish we did not need a book like *Between the World and the Urban Classroom*, but we do now more than ever. I am writing this foreword during a tumultuous time. It is a time when the rights of women, minorities, non-Christians, immigrants, students with disabilities, low-income families, and so many other groups are constantly being threatened.

The publication of this book coincides with Donald Trump, a tyrant, taking office as the 45th President of the United States and Betsy DeVos, an individual without any experience in public education, being confirmed as United States Secretary of Education. We cannot afford to be cavalier with our words or critiques because they can push and shift the dialog that may change the actions of those who think they are White and those who consume Whiteness, regardless of color. The contents of *Between the World and the Urban Classroom* could not more poignantly make this point.

Much love and light to everyone fighting for a better tomorrow, for equity and justice for Black and Brown youth in urban classrooms.

Bettina L. Love
Atlanta, GA
District 5

ACKNOWLEDGMENTS

They say it takes a village to raise a child. The same can be said of this book and we would like to acknowledge all the "villagers" who worked with us to get this book published. We are grateful to Michel Lokhorst from Sense Publishers who has offered support for this book ever since we pitched him the idea in 2012. We owe a debt of gratitude to the book's contributors who did an outstanding job on their respective chapters. Besides being easy to work with, they took our vision for this book and crafted critical and compelling works that are sure to draw readers in. We appreciate the time, energy, and thoughts of Bettina Love who wrote the foreword and Shirley Steinberg who wrote the afterword. We are privileged to call them colleagues and friends. We would like to offer our thanks to Jane Sinagub who did a tremendous job with the technical editing of this book. To Elham Ataeiazar whose exceptional artistic talent led to a cover that captures the essence of this book. Thank you to everyone else who has supported this book and who has helped raise the bar on our scholarship. Finally, a special thank you to everyone who reads this book and continues to strive for equity and justice in education, particularly for our nation's most vulnerable youth.

***

I would like to acknowledge my extraordinary wife, Alexis, and my two brilliant daughters, Grace and Juliet. Your unwavering support has been and continues to be everything. To my mother who suddenly departed this world in 2015, I love you! Pops, thank you for always pushing me to be better. To my sister and her family, thank you for always listening. I am blessed to have you all on my team.
 – George Sirrakos Jr.

To the ancestors, thank you for allowing me to be a vessel for our work.
 – Christopher Emdin

GEORGE SIRRAKOS JR. AND CHRISTOPHER EMDIN

INTRODUCTION

In *Pedagogy of the Oppressed*, Paulo Freire (2000), referring to "the radical," writes, "This individual is not afraid to confront, to listen, to see the world unveiled" (p. 39). In a global society with near unlimited access to news and information, the work of the educator is to be "the radical" that Freire speaks of. Now more then ever, the work of the educator is to peel back the layers of information that inhibit us from engaging in work that gets to the core of the major issues around urban education. Too many continue to see, and have become adjusted to, a veiled world—a world riddled with lies about everyone being treated equally and afforded the same opportunities. We have become a people who consume information at lightning speed, including information about sports, the economy, entertainment, the environment, politics, education, violence in our communities, and death. How often do we stop to think about these stories? How often do we ask ourselves, "What is there to learn from these occurrences?" "How is this affecting my teaching?" In this book, the editors have compiled a collection of nine critical essays that each examine a significant event or phenomenon. The purpose of each essay is to help readers see the world unveiled, through a more critical lens, and to problematize long held beliefs about urban classrooms, with regard to race, gender, social class, equity, and access.

We cast the title of this book, *Between the World and the Urban Classroom*, from Ta-Nehisi Coates's literary work *Between the World and Me* (2015). We do so, not only because of the timeliness of the text given the present racially charged cultural and political climate that both this book and Coates' text respond to, but because of the ways that the urban classroom is the central character in this text. In other words, we see the urban classroom as a living organism that inspires and requires cautionary narratives in order to be saved from the dangerous world it is a part of. In *Between the World and Me*, Coates writes a letter to his adolescent son explaining what it means to live in a Black body, both historically and in today's world. He expounds upon historical events and personal experiences, and through these narratives, unveils the realities around race and anti-Blackness in the United States. Similar to Freire's push to "see the world unveiled," Coates writes to his son, "I would not have you descend into your own dream. I would have you be a conscious citizen of this terrible and beautiful world" (p. 108). In this quote, Coates alludes to a desire for his son to have a heightened level of consciousness about the world and not live in a false reality or his "own dream." Contemporary education is built on false realities and unrealistic dreams about education that perpetuate the myth that what happens in the world outside of the classroom has nothing to do with what can be done within it. There is an existing belief that all things considered, placing the same teacher with the same training in front of a classroom of urban, suburban or rural youth should allow each of those students to perform at the same academic level because "education is the great equalizer", and the classroom is where that equalizing happens. This way of thinking launches the imagination in a dangerous way that leads to the belief in a false reality that our classrooms are free from bias because they are embedded in a post-racial world – where race is no longer a construct that we need be concerned with (Wise, 2010). This post racial-reality that urban classrooms are functioning under is in many ways a different form of "the dream" Coates hopes to steer his son away from. It erases historical and contemporary contexts that when ignored, ensure that unrealistic dreams give a false sense of security. It is this unrealistic dream that ensures that inequities persist that we hope to awaken the reader from through this text. The essays in this book uncover truths beyond the classroom that highlight the myriad micro and macrosystemic issues that function to keep entire groups of young people oppressed within classrooms.

Critical theory and culturally relevant pedagogy are the frameworks that bind the essays in this book. The intersection of the two gives the reader the opportunity to "analyze their own lived relations and experiences in a manner that is both affirmative and critical" (Giroux, 1997, p. 108). Furthermore, the essays in this book each undertake an explicit approach to naming oppression and addressing it in classrooms that informs an essential way forward in urban schooling. We speak collectively when we say that, as people with an interest in urban education, we need to be aware of things happening around the world. We need to understand them, analyze them, and leverage them in urban classrooms. The purpose for doing so moves beyond making superficial connections to content. Rather, such analyses serve as models for how to teach that when enacted, function to instill the necessary skills to be critical consumers, activists, and knowledge constructors in students. Similar to Coates's work, this collection of critical essays is the body of *our letter* to families, educators, administrators, policymakers, teacher educators, and others who have a stake in the success of students, primarily those from traditionally marginalized backgrounds, in urban classrooms.

THE JOURNEY

As 2011 came to a close, *Time* magazine revealed "The Protester" as their selection for "Person of the Year." One of the book's editors and chapter contributors, George Sirrakos Jr., recalls purchasing the magazine and sitting on a park bench completely intrigued by the magazine's selection. At the time, much of what he knew about global protests was rooted in the inconveniences they had caused him. The unrest in Egypt prompted him to cancel a long-awaited trip to Cairo and the Occupy Wall Street protesters in New York City occasionally disrupted his commute to work. Yet, reading that particular edition of *Time* magazine transformed him. Global protests were put on center stage, and some of the most prominent protesters were given a voice. As he read on, he became despondent and increasingly aware of the many unearned privileges afforded to him. His privilege caused him to view critical movements for change as inconveniences. This cover story reinforced just how unstable and unfair the world could be; but it also helped him realize how the world was changing. Perhaps his greatest realization of that day was just how little he knew about everything that was happening around him, whether at the local, national, or international level and how, despite his lack of knowledge about these events, how they inevitably affected him.

At the same time that George Sirrakos Jr. was working through the many local and global movements that affected him during the powerful year of the protester, Christopher Emdin was writing short thought pieces about the world writ large for an online news outlet. These pieces were intended to help readers examine how recent phenomena in the world writ large could be viewed more critically by drawing life lessons from them. The topics range from the use of body cameras by police to the Michael Brown shooting and did not necessarily focus on the implications of the topics on the classroom. The goal of these articles was to bring some attention to dimensions of news stories that have been erased from the public discourse, but that have a direct impact on urban communities, and inevitably, urban classrooms. The chaos in the world at the time that we were writing and thinking about the forgotten narratives that were trickling into our work in urban classrooms have since hit classrooms with a barrage of force that makes this book necessary.

In the years leading up to and including 2011, protests across the globe were rampant. No one could imagine that the actions of a few lay people would spark protests that would ultimately bring down dictators in Tunisia, Egypt, and Libya and topple regimes in Syria and Yemen. No one thought that the citizens of Mexico would rise up against the terror of drug cartels, that the people of Greece would march together to demand accountability from their leaders, or that Americans would protest income and class inequality by occupying public spaces across the United States. The series of protests and revolutions across northern Africa and the Middle East, which would become known as the Arab Spring, were particularly captivating. The editors of this book understood that, as a people, we were at an exciting point in our history—a time that demanded change. We are at that time in urban education where young people are demanding similar change across urban America; and it can be spurred into motion by educators who can generate new practice by being inspired to action by the powerful essays in this volume.

In pulling together the essays in this volume, we were repeatedly struck by the many similarities between the struggles of oppressed people across the globe and urban youth of color. These similarities moved us to start posing questions that connected these youth to groups as diverse as indigenous populations in the United States to silenced voices in the Middle East. These similarities moved us to pose questions such as "How was the oppressive, pre-revolution political climate in Egypt similar to the stifling structures found in many urban classrooms?" and "How can knowledge about the Arab Spring provide educators with an understanding of why students feel, think, and act certain ways in the urban classroom?" We used these questions and many others as guiding lights in our own exploration of how to better meet and serve the needs of urban students of color. In our fervor to continue developing ourselves as urban educators and teacher educators, we uncovered several published works that investigated the importance of incorporating culturally relevant events in instruction. However, these typically referred to the localized cultural experiences of students, and did not give the lessons to be gleaned from larger issues/events beyond the local context much credence. While there is, undoubtedly, value in incorporating such experiences, we were more deeply interested in the potential value that understanding of contemporary national and international events held in improving teaching and learning in urban classrooms.

It was at an education conference in 2012 where the editors decided to take up the task of writing such a book. We shared our vision with Michel Lokhorst at Sense Publishers who immediately embraced the idea. Eight weeks, several conversations, and one book contract later, we began the writing process. We gathered information and wrote on a range of topics, including the murder of Trayvon Martin, the financial crisis in Greece, the rise of Jeremy Lin as a New York Knick basketball player, and the Fukushima nuclear reactor disaster in Japan. Despite our progress, we felt that our analyses were lacking and simply not sufficient enough to accomplish the book's core purpose. A brief hiatus afforded us the realization that this project was too immense and significant to undertake alone. We endeavored to provide expert insights to various national and international events, yet we were limited by the fact that we did not possess such expertise. Rather than limit ourselves and our future readers to superficial analyses of the application of these events to urban classrooms, we decided to reach out to specific individuals who possessed the relevant and necessary expertise.

A COLLECTION OF CRITICAL ESSAYS

Despite the challenge of providing readers with robust analyses of timely events given the ever changing sociopolitical landscape we are embedded in, we remain pleased with our selection of authors and impressed with their respective contributions. We selected a diverse group of early-career and advanced-career scholars and asked these individuals to expand their current work by taking readers on a journey through a particular contemporary national and/or international event. This book is comprised of nine critical essays. Each essay, or chapter, has a two-fold purpose. First, by asking authors to think about their work in new ways, they offer the possibility of new insights into underexamined contemporary events through sociocultural, political, economic, racial, environmental, and/or gender viewpoints, for example. Second, as each author draws parallels between an event and urban classrooms, a better understanding of the microstructures and cultures that exist in urban classrooms emerges.

In Chapter 1, Arash Daneshzadeh uses the Black Lives Matter movement as a lens to explore the role of critical media literacy in decolonizing urban classrooms. In the next chapter, Venus E. Evans-Winters provides a sociopolitical critique of the recent violence against Black youth and adults at the hands of White vigilantes and state actors as a form of necropolitics. Further, Evans-Winters offers suggestions for how to utilize education to interrupt necropolitics and mediate racial oppression. In Chapter 3, Wayne Au looks at the growing movement against standardized testing, distinguishing between how urban test resistance differs from its suburban and rural counterparts. Further, this chapter uses the urban test resistance movement to identify specific lessons that can be learned about urban education more generally. In the fourth chapter, Treva Lindsey critically considers how racial and gender stereotypes are etched in conversations regarding the professional tennis player Serena Williams. Through a focus on Serena Williams, Lindsey explores how longstanding stereotypes about Black women continue to affect how people engage Black women and girls. The fifth chapter is written by one of the editors of this book, George Sirrakos Jr. In the chapter, Sirrakos uses ecological systems theory to better understand the Greek financial crisis and to challenge deficit perspectives of urban youth. Christopher Emdin who is also an editor of this book wrote Chapter 6. In the chapter, Emdin draws parallels between the spectacle of American politics vis-à-vis Donald Trump and the commercialized Hip Hop music industry to assert how urban classrooms are viewed as a spectacle, particularly by individuals who are external to them. In Chapter 7, Gloria Ladson-Billings urges readers to look at Hip Hop beyond beats, rhymes, and Beyoncé and explore it as a remix of culturally relevant pedagogy. In Chapter 8, Patricia Walsh Coates examines trends regarding both state and federal funding of sexuality education in the 21st century and the subsequent need for community-based programs for youth to make positive decisions regarding safe sex practices, with a specific focus on Philadelphia public schools. In the final chapter of this book, Mark Wolfmeyer highlights the need for urban education to emphasize the interrelationship between today's global crises, typically discussed separately as social injustice and environmental destruction, using Chicago's meat industry and the current Flint water crisis as examples.

As aforementioned, as editors, one of the problems we encountered was the swiftness with which news fades. An event can be considered news one day and an afterthought the next, as it drops out of mainstream media. While disappearance from the media does not make an event any less important, we were challenged with making sure that the events explicated in each chapter were significant enough to remain at the forefront of our readers' thoughts. As we complete this introduction and the editorial process, myriad other events have taken place. For example, the Zika virus outbreak in early 2016 showed how organizations could work together to protect citizens. During the 2016 Summer Olympics in Rio de Janeiro, Brazil, Ryan Lochte, a United States swimmer, showed the world that he could destroy private property, lie about it, and then use his White, male privilege and celebrity status to protect himself from any consequences. In October 2016, faculty across all

14 state universities in Pennsylvania went on strike for 3 days to protect the quality and integrity of their students' education. Currently, the Standing Rock Sioux Tribe along with other activists is vigorously protesting the construction of the Dakota Access Pipeline. The hashtag #NoDAPL has been trending for several months, uniting people across the world in solidarity for the rights of indigenous peoples. While we have not included these events, we encourage readers to use the same critical approaches and frameworks applied throughout this book to learn about them and apply those newfound understandings to urban classrooms.

As a final word, we would like to remind our readers of the need to interrogate society within the context of the urban classroom. Topics like the ones described throughout this book do not occur in a vacuum and neither do the transgressions of school-sanctioned trauma and violence against urban youth of color. Borrowing from the ideas of John Dewey (1938), schools and classrooms are a reflection of the world; therefore, in order to make sense of the urban classroom, we need to make sense of the world.

REFERENCES

Coates, T. (2015). *Between the world and me*. New York, NY: Spiegel & Grau.

Dewey, J. (1938). *Experience and education*. New York, NY: Simon & Schuster.

Freire, P. (2000). *Pedagogy of the oppressed* (30th anniversary edition). New York, NY: Continuum International Publishing Group.

Giroux, H. A. (1997). *Pedagogy and the politics of hope: Theory, culture, and schooling*. Boulder, CO: Westview Press.

Wise, T. (2010). *Colorblind: The rise of post-racial politics and the retreat from racial equity*. San Francisco, CA: City Lights Books.

ARASH DANESHZADEH

1. MEDIA AS CULTURAL DISCOURSE AND YOUTH EMANCIPATION

Do you determine
which thoughts you voice
or do they determine you?
What is the freedom you exercise
through speech?

– Saul Williams (2016), Songkeeper

The illiterate of the 21st century will not be those who cannot read and write,
but those who cannot learn, unlearn, and relearn.

– Alvin Toffler (1970), Future Shock

DECENTERING WHITENESS FROM SCHOOL-STUDENT POWER RELATIONSHIPS

Mobile social media has not only expanded the realm of possibility for remote communication and networking, but also new opportunities for education and resistance. In the movement for Black lives, galvanizing a critical mass of support is paramount to legitimizing a growing need for advocacy and dissent. In organizing dialectic for activism, educational scholars and direct-service practitioners at the grass-roots level become increasingly pivotal in providing tools for youth of color who are fed up with the violence imposed by a militarized police system. Literacy education and activism are intimately related, as students make sense of the messages peppered across a glowing screen. As students' lives are saturated with Eurocentric history that lacks nuance about the narratives of the Black and Brown diaspora, literacy emerges as instrumental to reading, interpreting, and producing counter-narratives to the apolitical and pathological stories of Black plight and demagoguery. Black Lives Matter anchors its resistance in counter-narratives. That is, a literacy education that creates a multidimensional and fluid interpretation of Blackness that is neither tethered to false White superiority nor codependent on ahistorical frameworks that position Black youth as ontologically criminal. Surrogates and members of Black Lives Matter chapters across the United States organize youth activists across immortalized time and cyberspace. They deftly utilize the dialogical momentum of a boundless Internet as unofficial pedagogues, providing erased

G. Sirrakos & C. Emdin (Eds.), Between the World and the Urban Classroom, 1–18.

narratives for youth in the throes of discovering their own radical psyche. In order to support a burgeoning migration of activism to the Internet, teachers in urban schools across America have a duty to provide unsanctioned space and tools for critical media literacy.

In citing Carmen Luke's (1994) deconstruction of the bridge between feminist theory and critical media literacy, Kellner and Share (2005) define critical media literacy as germane to school-level activism training:

> Feminist theory and standpoint epistemologies provide major contributions to the field of critical media literacy. For example, Carmen Luke (1994) combined cultural and feminist studies which allow for an "epistemological standpoint which acknowledges difference(s) of identity, the cultural constructedness of 'Theory', 'History, and 'Truth', and the cultural dynamics of our own labor as academic researchers and teachers" (p. 33). She linked a feminist political commitment to transformation with recognition of media misrepresentation and stereotyping. This required unveiling the political and social construction of knowledge, as well as addressing principles of equity and social justice related to representation. (p. 370)

This chapter explores the role of critical media literacy in urban classrooms. Specifically, I explore the relationship between activism that is fostered at the school and community level. The integration of media in school, by itself, does not enhance access to political discussion, only access to material-technological power. Finally, I historicize digital literacy education and describe its pitfalls and ability to leverage youth mobilization and amplify youth voices committed to advancing the movement to humanize and empower Black lives.

In May of 2016, a group of Black students at Wagner High School in San Antonio, Texas were suspended for "express[ing] themselves through what they wear" (Taylor, G., 2016, para. 3) during a fashion show by using garments they designed "to insist that Black Lives Matter" (Taylor, G., 2016, para. 3). Paradoxically, artists, including those mandated by school curricula like William Shakespeare and Maya Angelou, have commonly harnessed their creativity to serve as interlocutors of analytical commentary over myriad issues—social malaise and deeply polarizing current events in particular. The punishments meted by Wagner High School arrive on the heels of civic unrest across the United States resulting from numerous extrajudicial murders of Black citizens (and other racialized subgroups) by police and other law enforcement personnel. From Trayvon Martin and Terrence Crutcher to Rekia Boyd and Korryn Gaines, Black victims of police shootings were exposed through viral social media posts and other nontraditional syndicates. In the case of the suspended teens from Wagner High School, news of the suspensions was shared globally and soon thereafter, an outpouring of 1,700 signatures surfaced within an online petition that urged the school board to drop the suspensions and exonerate the teens. The students are sadly emblematic of a wider and historically sewn issue related to criminogenic hypersurveillance by public agencies (including schools).

These institutions uphold the tenets of White supremacy and settler colonialism under the guise of racial neutrality.

This chapter offers a critical perspective of urban school realities that cascade into the dispossession of historically dehumanized youth (e.g., those formerly incarcerated; LGBTQ; foster youth; homeless youth; immigrants/refugees; youth from Black, First Nation, and Latinx diasporas) from their intellectual ancestry and agency. By having a conversation unalloyed by normative ideals of commodification and decorum, I hope to enable community and public agency stakeholders to bend contemporary linear, deficit-based, and decontextualized frameworks of urban families and communities toward an ecological lens of urban schools. Understanding how contemporary urban schools reproduce hegemony can begin to forge solutions toward equity in our current system. This chapter draws from contemporary Black feminist scholarship, Hip Hop studies, as well as critical media literacy to harvest pluralistic approaches and unveil a radical glimpse into what decolonization can mean for urban schools in America.

It is a great irony that the very schools we uphold as paragons for youth interests and bastions of civic advancement, sanction Black youth for expressing a mantra as axiomatic as "Black Lives Matter." These institutions, much like Wagner High School, operate as racial enclosures (Sojoyner, 2013) and dehumanize youth, particularly Black, First Nation, and Latinx, students, by eliminating opportunities for self-directed protest. In her groundbreaking work, Simone Browne (2015) offers an insightful unpacking of the function of dehumanization by school-based professionals, known as *epidermal racial schema*, which accounts for the anxiety induced by historical ideology grounded by anti-Blackness that is aggressively supported by action arms of the state (i.e., K-12 schools). According to Browne, this *epidermalization* of students at Wagner High School heralds the "moment of fracture of the [Black] body from its humanness, refracted into a new subject position [of imminent threat or inferiority]" (p. 98). These school-based transgressions give stock to the necessity for critical pedagogy that abdicates from telling students what to think, but rather offers the conditions for unsanctioned expression by creating what scholars have called "third space" or "hybrid" educational sites (Gutierrez, Baquedano-Lopez, & Tejeda, 1999). These spaces are replete with tools for decolonization of primordial and colonial thinking. Additionally, third space schools transition from historically confining institutions to sites that promote "sociocritical literacy" (Gutierrez, 2008) or the fundamental understanding of how communities are transformed by inverse relationships between oppression and expression. Peter McLaren (1998) provides a powerful benediction to the critical literacy interwoven within schools determined to transform asymmetrical foundations of power in our society that repress the self-definition of youth, like the teens suspended by Wagner High School. Here, McLaren additionally notes about the dialectical model of critical knowledge building:

Preparing students for critical citizenship through critical literacy deepens the roots of democracy by encouraging students actively to participate in public discourses and debates over social, economic, and political issues that affect everyday life in their own and neighboring communities. In this way, students can acquire the pedagogical courage and moral responsibility to participate in democratic life as critical social agents, transforming themselves into authors of their own histories rather than being written off as the passive victims of history. In this regard, we would do well to remember the manifest possibilities offered by the creation of a socialist society, including those of education. (pp. 52–53)

In Mary Shelley's (1841) *Frankenstein*, a monster is tragically pieced together from what is illustrated as the bodies of society's wayward criminals. The quietly precocious mind of the stigmatized and nondescript specimen, built by Dr. Frankenstein is programmed as a passive vessel, without autonomy or legible voice. In Dr. Frankenstein's insatiable and self-aggrandizing pursuit of advancing medical canon, he confines the hulking and disfigured "monster" and deprives him of knowledge regarding his origins and any opportunity for self-expression. Tragically, the abominable creature at the center of Shelley's iconic tale resists and ultimately lends to the destruction of the lab and doctor from which he was conceived. This parable offers a potent and jarring analogy for the risks of circumventing human expression while simultaneously promoting one's own enlightenment. One message is abundantly clear: fostering an educational climate that promotes unalloyed self-definition, divested from the superimposed biases and programming of repressive forces, is fundamental to human longevity. The social proximity of power (Magee & Smith, 2013) embodied by the relationship between Dr. Frankenstein and the creature underscores the razor sharp link between justice and autonomous, or unsanctioned, expression. Consistent with this idea, is the notion that asymmetrical power, or power that aims at controlling others, produces asymmetric social distance, also known as social status.

Magee and Smith (2013) model balkanized differences in social distance as the basis for autocratic control. Social hierarchy undermines democracy. Leaders who punish dissent are legitimized by the institutions they steward. The interstitial role of ownership over one's own narrative plays an instrumental role in creating emancipatory conditions for living and learning. In this regard, narrative serves as a nucleus for power in the divide between—what critical race scholars describe as—subaltern (colonized) and majoritarian (dominant) populations (Delgado Bernal, & Villalpando, 2002).

Revolutionary scholar, Paulo Freire (1985), cautioned of ways that schools and other social institutions disconnect people from expression and self-determination—by commodifying youth as inanimate objects and binary code. This commodification masquerading as objectivity was on full display in *The Bell Curve*, by renowned eugenicists, Richard Herrnstein and Charles Murray (1994). In their controversial work, Herrnstein and Murray take the position that schools are flagships for social promotion, and the authors place the onus of disproportionate academic outcomes (i.e., truancy, retention, graduation) between subpopulations on the "cognitive differences in racial and ethnic groups" that are "inheritable between parents and children" and influenced by the intellectual "stunting" or stimulation of the environment (pp. 314–315). Of course, this is extraordinarily insulting considering 1,300 documented years of [global] chattel anti-Blackness and anti-indigeneity, forging the current racialized economy that continues to pulsate according to the impetuous whims of White racial framing (Ball, 2011; Feagin, 2006). *The Bell Curve* is also asynchronous with studies that disprove Darwinian pathologization of Black youth, as it is fraught with negative theorizations about urban schools that disproportionately serve Black students. It insinuates a litany of false binaries that associate intelligence with inherent ability rather than socially accepted demarcations of knowledge.

The collective denial, or racial "dysconsciousness" (King, 1991), embedded within eugenic pretenses percolated by Herrnstein and Murray (1994) and their ilk, fails to interrogate ecological systems that condition learning outcomes. Dysconsciousness bolsters what can be summarized as a sociological process of school chattelment, a more sizable and violent panopticon against youth. School chattelment refers to the institutionally backed assault against youth culminating from the process of rendering students of color and economically starved communities as school property. As a result, these youth become sociologically confined and programmed by way of a racialized-gendered demarcation. This codified value system regularly flies under the banner of "market-based" or "norm-referenced" rubrics for educational achievement. The process of school chattelment is devoid of human interests and ethical boundaries within society, and not exclusive to urban classrooms settings. Often, the vernacular of chattelment is inconspicuously lodged in deprivationist interventions, heralded by terms like "at risk youth" or "high-needs students," which are advanced by market-based school reforms aimed at promoting equality in urban classrooms. Terms like "at risk" label youth deemed unfit socially and academically in our current epoch of no-excuse education. Paradoxically, these deficit-based terms also sort youth by race, gender, and economic status. Deficit language is often a harbinger of school chattelment. It is through the restriction and appropriation of identity that students no longer act as autonomous agents, but rather inert vehicles that drive the disparate divisions of labor that exist within our society forward.

But dysconsciousness is merely one register of *The Bell Curve's* central argument. Herrnstein and Murray (1994) attempt to make causal correlations between *race* and "heritable transmission" (p. 314) of intelligence. Their argument, however, lacks a discussion of the active forces that position institutional and intergenerational *racism* as the symbiotic underside of seemingly objective and racially neutral school norms and values. Karen and Barbara Fields (2012) describe the racially deceptive alchemy of contemporary eugenicists as *racecraft*, a vanguard incarnation of colorblind ideology, which contorts race into a biologically determined trait rather than a racist precipitate of concentric social apparatuses. Overcoming the invisibilized albeit ubiquitous pretext of race—as an "ingredient of nature" (Fields & Fields, 2012, p. 128)—is no small feat. Fields and Fields (2012) suggest that youth of color from working-class communities, most vulnerable to racist assumptions regarding their abilities, must reclaim and become fully in "charge of their prose" in order to rewrite the "'religion' [of White supremacy and racial inferiority] as conventionally understood" (p. 242). This requires a more consistent and active role imbued by students (and their communities) in disrupting the ethos that drives their educational institutions. Freire (1976) succinctly captured the parasitic relationship between passive and active participation of pupils in academic institutions by distinguishing between students "being in the world" and "being with the world" (pp. 67–71).

Freire's (1976) bifurcated depiction of passive and active students in America's urban schools, exposes White supremacist notions of intellectual and cultural superiority within academic curricula. One way to divest school curricula from the racialized hierarchy that advances the mission of academic imperialism, is to draw upon the rich canon of Black feminist scholars. These scholars also inform the burgeoning field of critical media studies and Hip Hop pedagogy. Both fields are rapidly growing and can be harnessed to unearth the power paradigms that anchor both school and societal issues. These interloping power paradigms have been described as a web-like matrix of domination (Collins, 1990). Patricia Collins is a leading advocate of applying Black feminist theory to examine and deconstruct organizational issues. In the wake of state-sanctioned racial violence that plagues youth in urban schools, Afrocentric feminism calls for fostering a fundamental paradigmatic shift that,

> Rejects additive approaches to oppression. Replacing additive models of oppression with interlocking ones creates possibilities for new paradigms. The significance of seeing race, class, and gender as interlocking systems of oppression is that such an approach fosters a paradigmatic shift of thinking inclusively about other oppressions, such as age, sexual orientation, religion, and ethnicity. (Collins, 1990, pp. 221–238)

The dynamic between academic chasms and self-expression by students does not evade institutions of teaching and learning. Schools are financial, cultural, and social microcosms of larger power structures. The protected and towering social status of higher education has an inverse relationship with the subordinated and disenfranchised status of subgroups in various milieus of society—like those from economically blighted communities of color. The existential contradiction of schools is captured by Freire (1972) who explains that schools distort social injustices by codifying characteristics of dominant cultures—such as language and manufactured details of history—in order to mobilize a sense of aspiration and solidarity with the dominant class. In the following passage, Freire articulates the role of academic distortion upon the narrative of subaltern communities, stressing the following:

This distortion occurs within history; but it is not an historical vocation. Indeed, to admit of dehumanization as an historical vocation would lead either to cynicism or total despair. The struggle for humanization, for the emancipation of labor [from its relation with Capital], for the overcoming of alienation, for the affirmation of men as persons would be meaningless. This struggle is possible only because dehumanization, although a concrete historical fact, is *not* a given destiny but the result of an unjust order that engenders violence in the oppressors, which in turn dehumanizes the oppressed. (pp. 20–21)

Freire uses no uncertain terms in the parallel he draws between revisionist history (operating under the auspices of objectivity) and academically perpetuated violence. This violence is often subtle and casts an obfuscating shadow the size and shape of normative bell curves. These bell curves have been championed by eugenic scholars. They operate as vectors for incubation and reproduction of dominant ideology that govern power structures. In order to deconstruct infrastructures bent toward apartheid, from prisons to banks, schools must pivot their stance from ideological reproduction to dialogical interrogation and disruption of ideology. Critical pedagogy is inextricably related to justice work, as it aims to apply inquiry and critical analysis of institutional power to uproot registers of oppression from their historical bedrock.

DIALOGICAL RESISTANCE: MEDIA AS PROXY FOR CRITICAL LITERACY

The current model of educational management is primarily driven by an archaic edifice of market-based reforms grounded by financial expediency. This model of scientific management, which can be traced to industrialization, was theorized by Adam Smith's (1776) magnum opus, *An Inquiry Into the Nature and Causes of the Wealth of Nations*. Smith contends that differences in social status are "not products of nature, custom, or education," but rather an "effect of the division of labour" (p. 14). Smith attributes various strands of hierarchy imposed by wages and credentials as the ways in which a power structure maintains, clones, and communicates with itself. Taylorism is a modern term that encapsulates the historical legacy of scientific management and social Darwinism. Kenneth Gray (1993) describes Taylorism as, "the belief that the preordained and natural order of and the maximization of profit dictate that the fittest should manage as benevolent dictators and the rest should work" (p. 371). With regards to education, Taylorism has played a crucial role in signifying both status and outcomes, as the omnipresent ideology of capitalism governs a society of "minimal participation in decision-making by the majority (the workers)" and protects "a single minority of managers" (Bowles & Gintis, 1976, p. 2). The division of labor serves as a proxy of social power, particularly across racial lines. Inconsistent school funding and negligent appropriation of resources in predominantly Black communities from economically blighted neighborhoods have resulted in high teacher turnover and negative educational outcomes when measuring by national benchmarks for academic

7

achievement. It is imperative to acknowledge the unequal history of school funding in order to debunk the cozy myth of egalitarian opportunities in urban education.

In an open letter addressed, in part, to assuage the growing rancor of kindergarten through 12th-grade teachers who had grown disillusioned by a national trend toward Taylorism and rote standards of teaching, former Secretary of the U.S. Department of Education Arne Duncan (2011) wrote, "You rightfully believe that responsibility for educational quality should be shared by administrators, community, parents, and even students themselves" (para. 5). While honoring the autonomy of the teaching profession, Duncan's letter did not affirm that agency of its students, as active partners—with teachers—in the apparatus of instruction and curriculum design. In the letter, Secretary Duncan denotes several soft and technical skills that will be used to measure the effectiveness of high-quality education programs throughout the United States. Duncan's list was largely drawn from the National Education Association, which had previously identified four learning domains that govern the curricula of 21st century youth (Trilling & Fadel, 2009):

1. Global awareness and civic literacy.
2. Critical thinking, communication, collaboration, and creativity.
3. Media and information literacy.
4. Leadership, social responsibility, and cross-cultural skills.

These four criteria amass a breadth of knowledge that seeks to transform our society by capitalizing upon access to technology, digital arts, and preexisting funds of knowledge ("the historically accumulated and culturally developed bodies of knowledge and skills essential for household or individual functioning and well-being among students") (Gonzalez, Moll, & Amanti, 2005, p. 133). While bringing technology and technical education to a more diverse body of students is paramount to achieving the globalized classroom envisioned by the National Education Association, it is incumbent upon schools to reflect upon their current practices to ensure that students are prominently positioned to influence school leadership writ large. For the purposes of this discussion, school leadership is defined by three tiers of engagement with its constituents. Those tiers include *microsystemic* engagement with the individual student; *exosystemic* engagement with the community from which students derive, such as parents or guardians, spaces of intercommunial worship like mosques, or community-based or federal organizations that cater to historically marginalized students such as federal TRiO programs; and finally, *macrosystemic* engagement with the larger society that both politically and socially leverages the conditions that create the racial and class isolation of urban America's schools—this includes representatives from public and private agencies, including but certainly not limited to school board members, financial brokers, mental health experts, policymakers, and citizens at large. This three-tiered lens of school design draws upon the ecological systems theory developed by Urie Bronfenbrenner (1979). This theory explains that community engagement requires a partnership that surpasses the limitations of individual teacher-pupil relationships.

In his harrowing statement regarding the dual loyalties that exist among students from historically marginalized groups who attend schools concentrated with White supremacist values, Nicholas Hartlep (2013) testifies that "Whiteness wants [him] to be its pawn so that it can divide-and-conquer people of color. [His] choice is resistance through rejection and refutation of the passive, quiet, and sullen" (p. 68) student. There are ample voices that share the experiences of subtle and more palpable assaults on our consciousness. These assaults are soft coursing through the veins of a political education that aims at stratifying the norms of settler colonialism and migrating Black voices to the fringe. Without the globalized voices of students inculcated within academic leadership, which is fortified by a pillar of criticality, schools will simply reify the colonial project, which I refer to as the postmodern version of academic imperialism. Students are necessary agents to expose the blind spots in structure, the lacunas in narrative, and indict the inconsistencies between the mission of urban schools and the materialized, oft pernicious, outcomes.

There are many recent examples of schools attempting to bolster academic imperialism. In 2010, Arizona state legislature signed HB 2281 into law. This law banned ethnic studies in schools throughout Arizona and registered monthly fines for institutions that failed to comply with the sanction on Black, Asian American, First Nation, and Chicano studies classes (Phippen, 2015). During the fall of 2015, the Texas Board of Education adopted a resolution on curriculum that taught students, "Moses played a bigger role in inspiring the Constitution than slavery did in starting the Civil War" (Editorial Board, 2015, para. 1). Going "viral" in the millennial age, as the students at Wagner High School can attest, is not a benign process—but also serves as a harbinger of violence transgressions. However, in the epoch of populist scrutiny empowered by a virtually universal Internet, violence perpetrated by urban schools or imperialistic education policy is not beyond reproach or exposure. In a recent study by the Pew Research Center (2016), it was reported that almost two-thirds of Black social media users in the United States said that most or some of the posts they saw on the Internet were about racial issues. As a diametric contrast, a towering 70% of White social media users reported never seeing or posting anything related to race (Pew Research Center, 2016). This schism is indicative of an epistemological and dialectical connection between narrative and power. In the context of urban schools, students who are consigned to the fringe of society (e.g., Black working-class communities) rarely have their narratives centered in school. This virtual erasure compounds the physical assault on Black people by denying an opportunity to humanize and legitimize the reification of anti-Black and postmodern colonialism in schools. The approach to sociocritical linguistics promoted by Kris Gutierrez (2008) offers a lens for schools to magnify perspectives from student populations that had traditionally been outlawed in this country.

What does it mean to actively solicit perspectives from students in America's urban schools? How can scholar-activists use their praxis to curtail, much less uproot, the zeitgeist that underwrites the criminogenic architecture of school leadership? In nearly 2 decades as an educator, the rhetoric on school policy and organizational behavior continues to flummox my most ardently critical sensibilities. There is a growing dissonance that permeates the national conversation on urban school reform that channels the vanguard of participatory politics. That is, the conspicuous absence of youth, particularly Black working-class students. These children are left out by the morass of performance funding algorithms and academic norms as primary stakeholders in school decision-making processes. The ontological contradiction lies in national education reform movements uplifted by rallying cries like "student-centered curriculum" or culturally-sustaining pedagogy (Paris, 2012) that fails to generate a permanent, deeply ingrained and symbiotic relationship between community members (including students) and schools. While it would be hard pressed to argue that students are the cornerstone of an egalitarian future, they are all too often rendered as passive observers to a super-imposed literacy of schooling.

As an educator, the crux of my praxis centers upon disrupting systemic violence. There has long been a symbiotic relationship between the criminal justice system and public education in the United States (Kozol, 2005; Nocella, Parmar, & Stovall, 2014; Rios, 2011; Skiba, 2001). A conspicuous brand of youth control (Rios, 2011) and White-racial assimilation (Feagin, 2013) bridge these seemingly diametric social milieus. Since the earliest incarnations of American public schools, the dominant political narrative has contoured the shape of acceptable curricula. Dating as far back as the incipient era of settler colonialism, education has politically sanctioned the curriculum that affirms cultural identity. A legacy of historical dehumanization lives in today's education technocracy. Cultural determinism has dominated the epistemological and experiential lens in which students, particularly Black and indigenous youth, have viewed their intellectual ancestry. The machinations of cultural genocide, however, are not solely focused on physical extermination, but rather, on identifying and re-emphasizing power relationships between youth and academic institutions. The wizadry of racecraft, normalizing cultural erasure, reflects a psychological assault on a student's ability for self-identification. Racecraft (Fields & Fields, 2012) distinguishes between identity that is assumed by youth through their contextual interface with the world and the process of identification superimposed by institutions upon youth. This disequilibrium also exists between the scruples that schools—much like police departments—purport to uphold and protect and the deleterious outcomes associated with harsh discipline. Discipline is inextricably tethered to the myopic surveillance of Black youth whose ontology carries a scarlet letter of suspicion. The full extent of this suspicion is masked by the liberal multiculturalism of urban schools. That is, the notion that Black youth educators cannot partake and advance the mission of White supremacy. According to Keeanga-Yamahtta Taylor's (2016) rigorous account of resistance in the age of #BlackLivesMatter, Black educators and any other public officials can play a pivotal role in obscuring, "their actions under a cloak of imagined racial solidarity, while ignoring their role as arbiters of political power who willingly operate in a political terrain designed to exploit and oppress African American and other working-class people" (p. 79).

Fortunately, the advent of Facebook and Twitter has helped us to redefine our traditional notions around how people become educated. Learning doesn't just happen in a classroom. In order to reconstruct the definitions of liberatory learning, we must disabuse ourselves of the notion that liberation only occurs in the classroom. In my interview (2016) with David Turner, Berkeley Chapter President of Black Lives Matter, I explored the role of critical media in disrupting school-based violence:

Author: What, should be or can be, the role of critical media studies or Black Lives Matter in creating a counter-narrative to the White supremacist zeitgeist in schools?

Turner: I am a firm believer in developing a "critical eye" with youth. Most youth, especially historically marginalized youth, already have this, and their skepticism about the current state of affairs is optimal for developing what education scholars would call "critical consciousness." Critical media studies can play a key role in cultivating critical consciousness with you in several ways. If you simply play the media responses to the uprisings in Baltimore and Ferguson, and further dissect the political underpinnings of each, you can demonstrate the role of anti-Blackness in our current political climate. There are so many ways that educators can engage youth using critical media literacy, but they must be willing to adopt the tools that youth use, especially social media, to accomplish this.

Author: What should multicultural education learn from ideas championed by the BLM [Black Lives Matter] movement?

Turner: In the Black Lives Matter movement, we firmly believe that people have a deep knowledge of their own experiences, and their expertise in their own experiences should be the starting point of all political and cultural education. We believe that people have the right to exist and self-determine as their whole selves, and they all have the leadership potential to transform their conditions. With this being said, multicultural education could benefit from BLM movement by being more "people-centered." There is this notion that representation within curricula, or within the teaching force, or both is enough to transform the educational experiences of students of color, particularly Black students. This is not the case. One can have an Afrocentric curriculum at their school, and they can still be primarily anti-Black in their approaches to working with and loving on Black youth. Even in social justice circles, we rarely ask youth what they would like to see in their educational experiences, what they would like to learn, and how they want to see their struggles and successes represented in education. So, if multicultural education can learn from the BLM movement in any way, the people-centered component to it should change.

11

Author: What does your ideal classroom, or liberatory, learning space look like [as it pertains to ensuring an equitable and inclusive culture for Black youth]?

Turner: An ideal learning space is one that is created and maintained with the intention to be fully accessible to all of our youth's political imaginations. This means having the material resources (such as technology for quick searches and multimodal forms of learning) and this means having an educational experience that youth simultaneously help to cultivate and benefit from. The most liberatory learning spaces that I've seen had all of these components, and the learning was rooted in the students' experiences. This does not always look like Hip Hop pedagogy, while it can. But it definitely does not look like stealing from youth culture and educators of color to build a learning environment that others have been punished for building.

Author: In your experience, where do you believe schools are beginning to make sizable traction (if at all) in response to the emergent work of BLM? If not, then why do you believe many schools are still struggling to educate themselves to the critical discourse illuminated by BLM and others?

Turner: On an individual level, educators are making great strides incorporating aspects of the BLM movement into their classroom. Some high school teachers I've worked with use letter writing campaigns, youth participatory action research, database research, and even app creation as tools to engage in larger social movement work. Others have gone beyond their capacity as teachers and they took students to marches, to BLM meetings, and even to national convenings to bring their youth to the movement. I have also witnessed the opposite, where the students themselves will organize walkouts, have reinvigorated Black student unions, and have used the momentum of the movement to place demands on their institutions to become less "anti-Black." I think if we are going to be serious about committing ourselves to social justice and societal transformation, then being open to what Black youth have to say, as well as being in-touch with their "out of education" world, is key.

Author: How has neoliberalism's response to Black Lives Matter created further challenges for Black youth in school? How should education respond?

Turner: I think this problem is more complicated than just BLM. For example, the increased police presence in schools is a result of zero-tolerance policies that were necessitated because of high-stakes testing. We have seen school police body slam teenage girls and choke slam teenage boys all because of their Blackness. The privatization of schools also plays a big role, where "school culture" has become the model of creating success, and not the material deprivation that Black [and most times Brown] students experience in schools. So the neoliberal response to BLM, which has largely been couched in the politics of recognition, has become a major vehicle for domesticating Black resistance in and out of school context, across the K-16 spectrum. The first response I have would be aimed at policymakers and school districts, and I would tell them to fund schools with the children who have the least but need the absolute most. Second, I would encourage teachers and other educators to move away from disciplinary practices that criminalize our youth to practices that seek to heal them from racialized trauma that they experience both in and out of schools. In order to do that, however, educators need to be aware that it is happening in the first place. Finally, I would think that it is appropriate to develop activist identities with youth across the spectrum. Shawn Ginwright calls activism "radical healing" in his book, where youth can heal from their plagued social conditions by transforming them for themselves and their peers. These things are not "silver bullet" solutions, but they are ways to start addressing the political turmoil that neoliberal policies and practices have ravaged our schools within the last 2 decades.

During my interview (2016) with Karen Lewis, President of the Chicago Teachers Union, she provided a searing account of the potential for integrating the dialogical discussions of racial issues from social media into the classroom. She noted,

One of the best reasons to use critical media studies in schools is that it can be used very early in childhood. One cursory glance at any Disney film will show the villain is always dark. Always. Cinderella's stepmother, Ursula in the Little Mermaid, the vizier in Aladdin. You can ask young children who is good, who is bad, and how do you know? You can even approach the color issue in a variety of ways that will get them thinking. With older students, you can press further and ask how many hours of media viewing they've engaged in and how it has "colored" their perceptions of good and evil.

Popularly known as "hybrid" pedagogy, digital studies is an emergent field that combines strands of ethnic studies and critical pedagogy. It is not ideologically neutral, but rather seeks to promote safe cyberspaces unobstructed by the punitive metrics and policies of brick and mortar schools. Notable hybrid pedagogy scholar, Tim Monreal (2016) explains how urban schools entangled in the political and economic could benefit from clashing in more creative and critical ways with power paradigms:

In an education system that is increasingly going digital in everything from assessment to record-keeping, critical discussion about the role of digital practices should be a major feature in graduate schools of education. Without contestation or challenge, young teachers may assume digital technologies are immune to bias and inequality. I certainly fell into this category going through my graduate program. I wanted something that would engage my students immediately the next day in the classroom. My instructors were happy to introduce us to new tools, but I cannot recall one time where anything other than device or internet access was critically discussed. Power structures that may limit student/teacher agency and empowerment remain veiled, protected by the cacophonous voices (like mine) clamoring for practicality and innovation. (para. 4)

LIBERATING EDUCATIONAL SPACES VERSUS ERADICATING OPPRESSION

Social media provides an opportunity for critical teaching that underwrites transformative learning. It can invoke through testimony the first-hand accounts of Black youth of social injustice that "bears witness to our own historical disfiguration" (Felman & Laub, 1992, pp. 73–74). My first teaching post was 17 years ago at a continuation high school for students matriculating out of incarceration back into mainstream public high schools across California's Bay Area. While the circumstances surrounding their confinement were variegated, the actual offenses projected a certain level of paranoia on the part of schools that have shown to render substantial subjectivity on the part of administrators.

As technology further expands into sacred classroom spaces, so too grows the need for critical thinking and citation of empirically grounded conclusions. Without these skills, the line between opinion and fact could be further abstracted resulting in catastrophic proclamations about historically dehumanized children and their communities. Nonetheless, traditional tools, such as brick and mortar libraries and classroom discussions, have been replaced by social media chat rooms and electronic databases. These cyberspaces have staked their place at the epicenter of controversy as well. With the universal and immediate influence of social media, it is important to distinguish between those who act as covenants of collective research and advocacy, and those who only serve the interest of veiled funders and private conglomerations. The difference between meticulous research findings and casual opinion is complicated by the open source feature of the Internet in which "research" is readily made available by the common citizen for consumption by all. In this regard, technology turns self-proclaimed educators into messiahs and soothsayers. The concept of access to information and freedom are intertwined. Just because someone can present codified data and arcane analysis of focus groups, does not mean that their research is automatically reliable or statistically significant. Therefore, it is important that classrooms utilize their role as interlocutors with students, embracing the opportunity to help students shape their perceptions of reality by holding critical discussions, framed by historical connections, centered around the emergent activism, like the movement for

Black lives, which lives in fluid compartments of the Internet—from blogs to social media.

Racial enclosures, dysconscious racism, racecraft, and criminogenic surveillance of Black Lives Matter, in both online and physical school spaces, underscore a series of long-term battles in the war for school equity. There is no path toward educational justice that contains convenient detours around direct confrontations with injustice. The desperate search for these detours, often in the form of models, frameworks, or concepts that were not developed as paths to justice (e.g., colorblind ideology), is the greatest evidence of the collective desire among those who count on injustice to give them an advantage to retain that advantage. If a direct confrontation of injustice is missing from our strategies, initiatives, and movements, it means we are recreating the conditions we are pretending to want to destroy. This is the worst kind of injustice, cloaked in a phony manifestation of justice. Envisioning a school free of oppression is not a vision for freedom. Freedom is more than the absence of oppression in our urban schools. It is the opportunity and conditions requisite for self-definition. For example, Hip Hop education, popularized by scholar-activists like Murray Forman and Mark Anthony Neal (2012) as "Black language space" (p. 555), provides a site that is unsanctioned in its dialectical cypher and founded upon the love of land and respect for intellectual ancestry of its youth. Without creating a school modeled after a hybrid, or unsanctioned third space, classrooms run the risk of becoming what Jason Power (2011; better known as Elzhi from the Hip Hop group Slum Village) refers to as an urban "setup." In the claptrap where students are not active participants in leadership that resembles the democratic participation in a rap cypher, schools become a "glass house the devil throws stones through" (Power, 2011, para. 2). No vision for school-based justice can claim victory unless it encapsulates freedom for all youth. Freedom is not simply access to the Internet, but the opportunity to question and resist the ideology of disposability and the commerce of youth. By engendering critical race discussions in the classroom that broach the digital divide, schools can revise the constructs of community. Zeus Leonardo and Norton Grubb (2014) further explain, "because a school's existence is located in a web of other institutional forms," it requires a serious look at the "community's relationship with schools" (p. 55).

Tracing the genealogy of pain, one will usually find cultural erasure and suicide. Social toxicity and imperialism thread the fabric of school technocracy. If you're a journalist, your job is to be antagonistic toward power. It is not to be a defender of power's sense of propriety. In the same vein, critical literacy must include a visceral element of emancipatory journalism. Evoking critical race studies in the realm of digital storytelling is fundamentally important, argue Matias and Grosland (2016), as it "provides overarching critique of the hegemonic practices of Whiteness that often get overlooked or ignored due to the nature of its dominance" (p. 4). The world is permeable to change and adapts to our footprints. The classroom should be a fungible space. Therefore, discourse about the world must be mutually flexible. Imbibed from liberal postracial fantasy, schools have been able to propagate violence without much accountability or examination. No one is exempt in the confluence of youth-centered justice. In today's academic climate, there is a push toward "postracial" curriculum. This attempting of homogenizing school norms, controlling discourse around White middle-to-upper-class referents, and centering hegemonic narratives must become anachronistic in order to move urban schools toward an idealized vision of equity. Schools must explore the possibilities, challenges, and literacy practices of Black Lives Matter in the classroom. One example is the recent adoption of Black Lives Matter-related curricula in the San Francisco Unified School District. This constitutes a trove of literacy curriculum that spans numerous breadths of knowledge from ethnic studies to public policy that exposes K-12 students to issues that plague their communities in the most panoramically ecological sense. Schools in communities like San Francisco and Oakland must address how urban educators can confront the tensions of using a critically multicultural framework that addresses anti-Blackness in and out of historically monocultural classrooms. By doing so, we can begin to align the perception of schools, as safe and inclusive spaces, with the reality experienced in the everyday lives of students.

REFERENCES

Ball, J. A. (2011). *I mix what I like: A mixtape manifesto.* Oakland, CA: AK Press.

Bowles, S., & Gintis, H. (1976). *Schooling in capitalist America: Educational reform and the contradictions of economic life.* New York, NY: Basic Books.

Bronfenbrenner, U. (1979). *The ecology of human development: Experiments by nature and design.* Cambridge, MA: Harvard University Press.

Browne, S. (2015). *Dark matters: On the surveillance of Blackness.* Durham, NC: Duke University Press.

Collins, P. H. (1990). *Black feminist thought: Knowledge, consciousness, and the politics of empowerment.* Boston, MA: Unwin Hyman.

Delgado Bernal, D., & Villalpando, O. (2002). An apartheid of knowledge in academia: The struggle over the legitimate knowledge of faculty of color. *Equity & Excellence in Education, 35*(2), 169–180.

Duncan, A. (2011). *An open letter from Arne Duncan to America's teachers.* Retrieved from http://www.ed.gov/blog/2011/05/in-honor-of-teacher-appreciation-week-an-open-letter-from-arne-duncan-to-americas-teachers/

Editorial Board. (2015, July 6). How Texas is whitewashing Civil War history. *The Washington Post.* Retrieved from https://www.washingtonpost.com/opinions/whitewashing-civil-war-history-for-young-minds/2015/07/06/1168226c-2415-11e5-b77f-eb13a215f593_story.html?utm_term=.c17bef821796

Feagin, J. R. (2006). *Systemic racism: A theory of oppression.* New York, NY: Routledge.

Feagin, J. R. (2013). *The White racial frame: Centuries of racial framing and counter-framing.* New York, NY: Routledge.

Felman, S., & Laub, D. (1992). *Testimony: Crises of witnessing in literature psychoanalysis and history.* New York, NY: Routledge.

Fields, K. E., & Fields, B. J. (2012). *Racecraft: The soul of inequality in American life.* London, England: Verso.

Forman, M., & Neal, M. A. (2012). *That's the joint: The hip hop studies reader.* New York, NY: Routledge.

Freire, P. (1972). *Pedagogy of the oppressed.* Harmondsworth, England: Penguin.

Freire, P. (1976). *Education: The practice of freedom.* London, England: Writers and Readers Publishing Cooperative.

Freire, P. (1985). *The politics of education: Culture, power, and liberation.* Westport, CT: Greenwood Publishing Group.

Gonzalez, N., Moll, L., & Amanti, C. (2005). *Funds of knowledge: Theorizing practices in households, communities, and classrooms.* Mahwah, NJ: Erlbaum Associates.

Gray, K. (1993). How we will lose: Taylorism in America's high schools. *The Phi Delta Kappan, 74*(5), 370–374.

Gutierrez, K. D. (2008). Developing a sociocritical literacy in the third space. *Language, Literacy, and Motivation, 43*(2), 103–198.

Gutierrez, K. D., Baquedano-Lopez, P., & Tejeda, C. (1999). Rethinking diversity: Hybridity and hybrid language practices in the third space. *Mind, Culture, and Activity, 6*(4), 286–303.

Hartlep, N. D. (2013). I refuse to be a pawn for Whiteness. In C. Hayes & N. D. Hartlep (Eds.), *Unhooking from Whiteness: The key to dismantling racism in the United States* (pp. 57–70). Rotterdam, The Netherlands: Sense Publishers.

Herrnstein, R. J., & Murray, C. (1994). *The bell curves: Intelligence and class structure in American life.* New York, NY: Free Press Paperbacks.

Kellner, D., & Share, J. (2005). Toward critical media literacy: Core concepts, debates, organizations, and policy. *Discourse: Studies in the Cultural Politics of Education, 26*(3), 369–386.

King, J. E. (1991). Dysconscious racism: Ideology, identity, and the miseducation of teachers. *The Journal of Negro Education, 60*(2), 133–146.

Kozol, J. (2005). *Shame of the nation: The restoration of apartheid schooling in America.* New York, NY: Crowe.

Leonardo, Z., & Grubb, W. N. (2014). *Education and racism: A primer on issues and dilemmas.* New York, NY: Routledge.

Luke, C. (1994). Feminist pedagogy and critical media literacy. *Journal of Communication Inquiry, 18*(2), 30–47.

Magee, J. C., & Smith, P. K. (2013). The social distance theory of power. *Personality and Social Psychology Review, 17*(2), 158–186.

Matias, C., & Grosland, T. J. (2016). Digital storytelling as racial justice: Digital hopes for deconstructing Whiteness in teacher education. *Journal of Teacher Education, 67*(2), 1–13.

McLaren, P. (1998). *Life in schools: An introduction to critical pedagogy in the foundations of education* (5th ed.). Boston, MA: Pearson.

Monreal, T. (2016, August 23). Beyond surface-level digital pedagogy. *Hybrid Pedagogy: A Digital Journal of Learning, Teaching, and Technology.* Retrieved from http://www.digitalpedagogylab.com/hybridped/beyond-surface-level/

Nocella, A., Parmar, P., & Stovall, D. (2014). *From education to incarceration: Dismantling the school-to-prison pipeline.* New York, NY: Lang Publishing.

Paris, D. (2012). Culturally sustaining pedagogy: A needed change in stance, terminology, and practice. *Educational Researcher, 41*(3), 93–97.

Pew Research Center. (2016). *Social media conversations about race.* Retrieved from http://www.pewinternet.org/2016/08/15/social-media-conversations-about-race/

Phippen, J. W. (2015, July 19). How one law banning ethnic studies led to its rise. *The Atlantic.* Retrieved from http://www.theatlantic.com/education/archive/2015/07/how-one-law-banning-ethnic-studies-led-to-rise/398885/

Power, J. (2011). *Detroit state of mind* [Record by Elzhi]. On Elmatic [LP]. Los Angeles, CA: The JAE.B Group.

Rios, V. (2011). *Punished: Policing the lives of Black and Latino boys.* New York, NY: New York University Press.

Shelley, M. (1841). *Frankenstein; Or, the modern Prometheus.* New York, NY: Pearson Longman.

Skiba, R. (2001). *Zero tolerance, zero evidence: An analysis of school disciplinary practice.* Bloomington, IN: Indiana Education Policy Center, Indiana University.

Smith, A. (1776). *An inquiry into the nature and causes of the wealth of nations.* London, England: Methuen and Company.

Sojoyner, D. M. (2013). Black radicals make for bad citizens: Undoing the myth of the school-to-prison pipeline. *Berkeley Review of Education, 4*(2), 241–263.

Taylor, G. (2016, May 20). Students suspended over Black Lives Matter signs garner support from across the globe. *Atlanta Black Star.* Retrieved from http://www.dignityinschools.org/news/students-suspended-over-%E2%80%98black-lives-matter%E2%80%99-signs-garner-support-across-globe

Taylor, K. Y. (2016). *From #BlackLivesMatter to Black liberation.* Chicago, IL: Haymarket Books.

Toffler, A. (1970). *Future shock.* New York, NY: Random House.

Trilling, B., & Fadel, C. (2009). *21st century skills: Learning for life in our times.* San Francisco, CA: Jossey-Bass.

Williams, S. (2015). *US (a.).* New York, NY: Gallery Books.

Arash Daneshzadeh
University of San Francisco

VENUS E. EVANS-WINTERS

2. NECROPOLITICS AND EDUCATION

Hence, to kill or to allow to live constitute the limits of sovereignty, its fundamental attributes. To exercise sovereignty is to exercise control over mortality and to define life as the deployment and manifestation of power.
– Achille Mbembe (2003)

With the rise of social media, the public has been bombarded by media clips of people of African ancestry being assaulted or gunned down in their own communities. However, the most controversial and emotionally charged media coverage includes images and commentary that cover the killing of young Black people at the hands of White citizens, in particular, White men. The most publicly viewed killings of Black citizens at the hands of White male citizens are the murders of Oscar Grant, age 22 (Oakland, California), Trayvon Martin, age 17 (Sanford, Florida), Renisha McBride, age 19 (Detroit, Michigan), Jordan Davis, age 17 (Satellite Beach, Florida), Tamir Rice, age 12 (Cleveland, Ohio), Michael Brown, age 18 (Ferguson, Missouri), Eric Garner, age 43 (New York), Freddie Gray, age 25 (Baltimore, Maryland), and Terrence Crutcher, age 40 (Tulsa, Oklahoma). There are assaults on and killings of Black bodies publicly displayed almost daily.

Because it is so common for Black citizens to be gunned down by White (male) authority figures (i.e., police officers) and White vigilantes (i.e., everyday citizens who believe that they or their communities need protection from the dangerous Black body), the purpose of this work is not to provide an overview of those murders. The purpose of this chapter is to provide a political context in which Black murders at the hands of White vigilantes and state actors are commonplace and normalized by both Whites and often non-Whites alike. White-on-Black violence is not considered abnormal in the U.S. context. It is argued here that many previous analyses have failed to look at the relationship between physical location, White racial dominance politics, and systems (and instruments) that serve to control and surveil the Black body and justify the murder of Black human beings. Assumptions of where people socially and physically belong serve as territorial markers for policed domains.

COLONIZED BODIES

I draw from Robert Blauner's (1969) notion of *colonization* and Achille Mbembe's (2003) conceptualization of *necropolitics* to attempt to explain White (male) adult violence against Black citizens. Throughout the chapter, I asseverate that

G. Sirrakos & C. Emdin (Eds.), Between the World and the Urban Classroom, 19–33.

White-on-Black violence is intentional, sanctioned, and normalized by policy, institutions (e.g., media, education, religion, judiciary), and the popular imagination. For the purposes of this chapter, Blauner's distinction between colonization and colonialism is most useful. In Blauner's article, "Internal Colonialism and Ghetto Revolt," the theorist describes colonization as a process and views colonialism as a social, economic, and political system. The theorist views the African/Black American experience as a colonization context outside of a colonial system or what Blauner refers to as internal colonialism.

Black Americans are descendants of enslaved people (and/or descendants of recent immigrants). Enslaved Africans were brought to North America, which was a land already inhabited by indigenous groups—culturally, economically, and politically. The Europeans colonized both the indigenous of North America and enslaved Africans. However, North America was a foreign land geographically, culturally, linguistically, economically, and politically to African people as opposed to indigenous North Americans. By the time Africans arrived in North America, Europeans had already begun processes of colonization of the indigenous people of Africa and North America. Africans in America became internal colonial projects.

In reference to the coined idea of internal colonialism, Blauner (1969) admits that as "problematic and as precise as it is, it gives hope of becoming a framework that can integrate the insights of caste and racism, ethnicity, culture, and economic exploitation into an overall conceptual scheme" (p. 394). Although arguably *colonialists* do not occupy the geographical or indigenous lands of Africans in America (notwithstanding gentrification patterns in many urban communities today), European Americans (or Whites) continue to control the educational, political, and economic conditions of African descended people in the US. Below, I demonstrate how Black people in America are colonized people in their own land. Blauner explains that there are four basic components of colonization:

1. Colonization begins with a forced, involuntary entry.
2. There is an impact on the culture and social organization of the colonized people as a result of the colonizing power carrying out policies that serve to constrain, transform, or destroy indigenous values, orientations, and ways of life.
3. Colonization involves a relationship by which members of the colonized group tend to be administered by representatives of the dominant power. There is an experience of being managed and manipulated by outsiders in terms of ethnic terms.
4. Racism is a system of domination. Racism is a principle of social domination by which a group seen as inferior or different in terms of alleged biological characteristics is exploited, controlled, and oppressed socially and psychically by a superordinate group (p. 396).

For the purposes of this chapter, the concept of colonization is applied to African Americans across a variety of communities, not simply urban areas, as was the case in Blauner's framework, for whether a Black person lives in an urban area or not,

Black people are often stereotyped as belonging in an "urban" area. In fact, the term urban has become synonymous with Black and Brown people. In the 1960s and 1970s, relying upon the popular imagination and scientific racism, politicians, business leaders, and suburban developers began to adopt the term "urban" to describe ethnically, linguistically, economically, and culturally diverse individuals and families residing in metropolitan area communities (see Augustine, 1991; Buendía, 2011; Buendía & Ares, 2006; Massey & Denton, 1993; Ward, 2004; Wilson, 1996 for further discussion on the social construction of urban spaces and population groups).

As articulated by Buendía (2011), "We have witnessed a collapsing of the spatial and the ontological of the space and racial and classed subject through the use of the conceptual proxy, or stand-in, urban" (p. 4). In comparison, the U.S. Census Bureau definition of urban areas moves beyond geographical locations to a conceptualization that considers the population density of any given area. For example, according to the U.S. census, urbanized areas contain 50,000 or more people, and urban clusters have a population of at least 2,500 to less than 50,000 people (U.S. Census Bureau, 2015). These definitions are rarely taken into consideration in public discourse or even in social science studies, like education (Buendía, 2011). The dangerous urban Black (male) trope is as common in national media as it is in scientific research and political discourse.

Although the majority of Black people continue to be segregated in high poverty and working-class majority Black high-density neighborhoods (Orfield, Kucsera, & Siegel-Hawley, 2012), it is fair to conclude that Black Americans have gained access to residential spaces (e.g., suburbs) traditionally reserved for Whites. Nonetheless, the US remains racially and economically segregated socially and physically. With this in mind, Blauner's (1969) conclusion that Blacks in America are colonized people can be applied to the social and political conditions of Black people today as well as be connected to their social vulnerability. Black people are socially vulnerable because outsiders dictate political and economic policies (e.g., schooling and media) that serve to govern their behavior and thoughts.

FORCE AND INVOLUNTARY ENTRY

First of all, Africans entered this continent as an enslaved labor force. After slavery was abolished, the majority of Blacks were forced into sharecropping the lands of Whites and pigeon-holed into domestic labor in White households. Then, if Blacks attempted to escape the social, political, and economic exploitation of the South, they were jailed, maimed, raped, or killed. Both Blacks in the North and South of the country were forced into racially segregated work and residential spaces (Feagin, 2014; Katznelson, 2005; Trotter, 1991). As a racial/ethnic minority in this country, Black people were brought involuntarily to this country by White colonialists and later forced into a subordinate racial and class status.

In other words, descendants of slaves entered this country by force, giving them a distinct designation as racial minorities and outsiders for centuries. Black youth in the US are only approximately 150 years post the abolition of slavery and 60 years past the end of Jim Crow practices in this country. Nonetheless, they live and are schooled in the midst of the prison industrial complex, or what Michelle Alexander (2010) refers to as "the new Jim Crow"—a racially and economically mass incarceration process that filters young poor Black and Brown males and females into the prison system.

Undoubtedly, Black youth have inherited a nation that cannot get past viewing their bodies as animals and work machines. Borrowing from Blauner (1969), I proclaim that colonized people's culture and social organization are shaped early on by "the colonizing power carrying out policies that serve to constrain, transform, or destroy indigenous values, orientations, and ways of life" (p. 396). Thus, the everyday realities of young Black people are directly affected by school policies, urban policing policies, and city government education and housing policies. Below, I briefly outline the most blatant formal and informal policies that affect youth at the interpersonal (micro) and community (meso) levels throughout childhood and early adulthood.

POLICIES THAT CONSTRAIN

Historical policies and practices, such as the enslaved not permitted to read, lynch laws, Jim Crow laws, and de facto segregation laws among many other written and unwritten laws, shaped the social and material conditions of Blacks in the US. Along with the historical *Brown v. Board of Education* (1954) decision, more recent policies, such as frisk-and-search and zero tolerance policies in schools, serve to surveil, control, and punish young Black bodies.

On the surface, *Brown v. Board of Education* (Warren, 1954) discontinued segregation of education based on race in the US when the Court declared separate was inherently unequal. However, this same legal decision led most school districts to dismantle Black-only schools and fire and prevent the hiring of Black teachers (Anderson, 1988; Bell, 1992; Siddle Walker, 1996). By systematically dismantling schools that served Black students and destroying the Black teacher profession, the nation began a legacy of deculturalization practices (Spring, 2016). Deculturalization practices in schooling attempt to strip African American children of their culture and replace it with the culture of the White middle class/oppressor or what is considered normative.

Deculturalization processes in education include replacing Black teachers and administrators with White female teachers and administrators (we see this more with the rise of corporate funded private and charter schools that actively recruit nonformally trained teachers outside of university teacher preparation programs); marginalizing Black students' cultural traditions at school by implementing a curriculum that is reflective of the dominating group's culture and history; and ridiculing, reprimanding, or penalizing Black children for speaking in their own language or dialects. I asseverate here that educational systems in the US are colonized spaces that serve to sustain and proliferate White supremacy and result in apartheid schooling that intentionally cements Black people to the bottom of the economic structure due to lowered expectations, culturally disconnected standardized curriculum and testing, inequitable school funding, poorly prepared teachers, and harsh discipline policies.

As explained by Smith (1988) in the *Harvard Law Journal*, many Whites were opposed to school integration; thus, policies and practices were put into place to control and manipulate Black students. For example, after *Brown v. Board of Education* (1954), Black children systematically endured corporeal punishment, were labeled as emotionally and behaviorally disturbed, diagnosed as having a learning disability, and suspended and expelled from school (Howard, 2013; Moody, 2016; Smith, 1988). Black boys were disproportionately disenfranchised by the public educational system post de jure segregation. Today, research shows that African American boys are suspended and expelled at higher rates than all other students, and African American girls have higher rates of suspension than all other student groups, except for their Black male counterparts (Crenshaw, Ocen, & Nanda, 2015; Morris, 2016). In fact, recent research suggests that Black students receive harsher punishments than non-Black students for similar behaviors at school (Elias, 2013; Moody, 2016).

Today, zero tolerance school policies disproportionately affect Black students (Hoffman, 2014). Although the majority of mass school shootings have occurred in predominately White communities at the hands of White males, Black and Brown students from lower-income school communities have mostly been impacted by zero tolerance policies. Directly after the *Brown v. Board of Education* (1954) decision, the expulsion and suspension rate of Black youth, which was virtually nonexistent before the Court decision, dramatically increased due to racial discrimination by White teachers and administrators. These policies lead to what has been referred to as the school-to-prison pipeline. For far too many Black youths, their first encounter with the criminal justice system occurred after a report by school officials to police authorities. The implicit and explicit message sent to many youngsters of African descent is that their presence is intolerable and reprehensible. Zero tolerance policies allow White authority figures and other outsiders of youth culture to control and surveil young people's bodies.

A contemporary example of a policy that serves to control and interrupt the daily lives of young Black people is stop-and-frisk. The stop-and-frisk policy in New York, for example, was a law that allowed local police officers to stop any individual in New York at random and search their person for possible illegal contraband, like drugs or weapons. According to an analysis by the New York Civil Liberties Union (n.d.), "innocent New Yorkers have been subjected to police stops and street interrogations more than 4 million times since 2002" (para. 2), and African American and Latino communities were primarily and disproportionately the targets of such stop-and-frisk practices ("Stop-and-Frisk Campaign," n.d.).

Interestingly, nearly nine out of 10 stopped-and-frisked New Yorkers have been completely innocent ("Stop-and-Frisk," n.d.). Despite a trend of innocence and noncriminal behavior among most Black and Latino youth who have been the target of stop-and-frisk policies, similar policies have been spreading in other major cities with the intent of disrupting and constraining the normal daily life and progress (e.g., walking on the streets to work, driving in a car to a family event, gathering on the corner with friends, going to school) of poor and working-class Black and other non-White people, while solidifying a climate of White authority and superiority (e.g., a police officer can interrupt your behavior or thinking without cause or warning). The intent is to invoke fear and intimidation between authority and those they are aiming to oppress with the constant reminder of White power.

Thus, stop-and-frisk policies have psychological and physical consequences. Stop-and-frisk and similar policies (e.g., the stand-your-ground laws) are reflective of slave codes, where Black people could be randomly stopped by White people and told to show their freedom papers or letters of permission to leave their enslaver's property. Random searches (and other owner-slave like policies) that keep the dominating culture in positions of power and authority and keep the colonized group in positions of subordination are the condition of the colonized. The above tactics are also present in urban school environments. Urban students are schooled to comply with the criminalization of their bodies through random lockdowns, metal detector walk-throughs, locker and property searches, and drug tests on public school campuses.

COLONIZED AND COLONIZER RELATIONSHIP

Blauner (1969) explains that colonization involves a relationship by which members of the colonized group tend to be administered, managed, and manipulated by representatives of the dominant power. As already stated, the majority of African American children will spend the majority of their school years learning at the feet of White (mostly female) teachers (National Center for Education Statistics, 2013). More than likely, these teachers have had little or no previous experience in Black communities or serving racial/ethnic minority students (Delpit, 2006; Gay, 2012). Furthermore, as is known with the schooling process, teachers teach their culture and their perspectives of the social world. Sadly, due to lack of cultural awareness on the part of White teachers, many children of color will learn White middle-class culture and only a White person's perspective of the social world.

Of course in the US, police officers—mostly White males—represent the most symbolically powerful group of state agents who enter into Black neighborhoods as enforcers of law and order. Men who "police" began as a voluntary vigilante group in the northern region of the US and in the southern region of the country, and such policing began as a method of intimidating, controlling, and tracking down enslaved Africans. Police officers were referred to as the "slave patrol." According to Potter (1995), slave patrols had three primary functions: (a) to chase down, apprehend, and return runaway slaves to their owners; (b) to provide a form of organized terror to deter slave revolts; and (c) to maintain a form of discipline for slave-workers who were subject to summary justice, outside of the law, if they violated any plantation rules.

After the abolishment of chattel slavery, and with the growth of urban cities, police officers began to take on the role of maintaining "social control" (Potter, 1995). Thus, police historically have enforced the rules, regulations, and laws of the White dominant class onto Black bodies. This historical perspective is important because it demonstrates that in the public imagination the role of police officers is to control Black people and urban populations, and in the Black imagination police officers should be feared. In the 21st century, White officers are overrepresented and Black officers are underrepresented in the majority of city police departments, even in cities that are majority African American (Ashkenas & Park, 2014).

RACISM AS A SYSTEM OF DOMINATION

Racism in the US is evasive and pervasive (Bell, 1992; Delgado & Stefancic, 2000). Much of the founding philosophy of the country was based on the continual rationalization and justification of the enslavement of Black people and colonization (or genocide) of Native Americans (Mills, 1997). As recent as the late 1800s to mid-1900s, scientists, university professors, and philanthropists used pseudoscience to attempt to establish scientifically the biological, intellectual, and cultural inferiority of Black people (Gould, 1996; Selden, 1999). The time period of the search and validation of the establishment of the superiority of Whites and inferiority of non-Whites is referred to as the eugenics movement. Eugenics science influenced the field of education more than any other institution, primarily through standardized tests and curriculum (Winfield, 2007). Although Eugenics as a formal science has disappeared from the mainstream, its ideas remain a part of the public imagination. Popular belief is that Black Americans are aesthetically, intellectually, morally, and culturally inferior to Whites.

For example, it is common knowledge that racism and violence have established their roots into all levels of education (Anderson, 1988; Siddle Walker, 2001; Watkins, 2005; Winfield, 2007; Woodson, 1990). Racism rested upon the belief that Blacks were (a) not deserving of an education, (b) uneducable, and (c) would forget their "place." Education is the most subversive way, through curriculum, pedagogy, language, discipline, and other policies, to convince Whites that they are superior and non-Whites that they are inferior. Content in schools covers White history and perspectives of the social world, pedagogy centers Whiteness and a White worldview, language of instruction is middle-class White English, and discipline and punishment are theorized and implemented from a White middle-class belief system (see Delpit, 2006; Gay, 2010; Irvine, 1990). Most would agree that racism in the US is less overt and has become more covert. Psychologists refer to covert forms of racism as racial microagressions.

Racial microaggressions are subtle forms of racism that are described as intentional and unintentional verbal, derogatory, or racial insults (Sue et al., 2007). Microaggressions have a significant impact on the psychology of the individual victim as well as on society as a whole. As is evident in patterns of residential racial segregation, education disenfranchisement of African Americans, and racial discrimination in employment, racial discrimination is not inscribed overtly in public law, but it is certainly enacted as common practice in subtle behaviors and attitudes toward Blacks. For me, the overrepresentation of Black men and women in prisons is also evident of a political, judicial, and economic system that systematically sets out to maintain the domination of Black people.

NECROPOLITICS

In response to Michel Foucault's conceptualization of biopower, Achille Mbembe (2003) raises the following questions:

> But under what practical conditions is the right to kill, to allow to live, or to expose to death exercised? Who is the subject of this right? What does the implementation of such a right tell us about the person who is thus put to death and about the relation of enmity that sets that person against his or her murderer? … Imagining politics as a form of war, we must ask: What place is given to life, death, and the human body (in particular the wounded or slain body)? How are they inscribed in the order of power? (p. 12)

Black people in the US are a group who were a colonized (and enslaved) people, brought to a colonized land (i.e., North America), and 400 years later are continually controlled and surveilled by the descendants of their colonizers. Black people reside in racially and economically segregated communities. As discussed in the previous section, in these isolated social and geographical urban milieus, social control is maintained through the educational (e.g., policing in schools and psychological warfare) and judicial (e.g., policing and mass incarceration of Black and Brown poor people) systems.

Mbembe's (2003) questions are answered based on the premise proclaimed in the above paragraph. Under what practical conditions is the right to kill, to allow to live, or to expose to death exercised? Those urban and sub-urban communities where Black people reside are prototypes of social, political, and physical control. When Black and Brown people deviate, or are made to appear as social deviants, then they give up their right to live. In juxtaposition, White state actors and vigilantes are given the right to kill the deviant Black body. It is appropriate to ask here, "Who is the subject of this right to live and to kill?" Through education policies and other social welfare policies (e.g., zero tolerance policies, White teachers and social workers), judicial policies (e.g., Jim Crow laws, discrimination in housing policies, stop-and-frisk), and the media, all U.S. citizens are socialized to view the Black body as deviant and White bodies as (moral) saviors.

Again, state and national governments have put these systems and guardians of law and order in place to protect the interest of "the people." In 2016, when U.S. Republican presidential candidate Donald Trump was asked to state his position on police killings against Black American citizens, Trump responded that cities needed to reinstate "law and order" and actively support police officers. In Trump's view and that of his supporters, there is not enough control in metropolitan areas and police officers are victims of so-called criminals. In the US popular imagination, cities are rampant with criminals lurking around every street corner. Political rhetoric like Trump's and other politicians' serves the purpose of putting citizens on alert, both potential victims and vigilantes. This call of alert is in fact a form of *necropolitics* that politicians and the media play a role in proliferating and sustaining.

Next, Mbembe (2003) raises the following question, "What does the implementation of such a right tell us about the person who is thus put to death and about the relation of enmity that sets that person against his or her murderer?" If we look at the countless Black people who have been put to death by White people, we learn that Black men's and women's lives are of less value than those of their White counterparts. Even at closer glance, we know too that Black youth are not viewed as children in need of state or adult protection in ways that White children are in this country. The message that too many young Black people receive is contain them or destroy them before they grow into adult urban predators. Consequently, Black youth are depicted in media and other social institutions as social problems in need of proper cultural and moral guidance. In schools, Black youth behaviors are perceived as more threatening to the school environment; thus, harsher consequences for typical adolescent behavior are administered to them.

In the US, Whiteness is associated with *law and order*, while Blackness is associated with unlawfulness and disorder. Enmity is the result of Whites viewing themselves as the natural citizens of the US and all others as tolerated second-class citizens whose rights can be taken away at any time if they fail to "stay in their place." In actuality, urban milieus are tolerated places. Therefore, if we respond to Mbembe's (2003) probe, "Imagining politics as a form of war, we must ask: What place is given to life, death, and the human body (in particular the wounded or slain body)? How are they inscribed in the order of power?" (p. 12), then we must admit that the dead Black body has become a symbol of White power. In the US, White Americans have sovereignty over Black Americans in theory (the popular social imagination) and in practice (i.e., little or no punishment for Whites who kill Blacks). Consequentially, the dead Black body—viewed over and over again in visual and social media—is comprehended by witnesses as simply contraband of war.

The viewing of the dead body over and over again across various mediums and time serves to (a) desensitize the populous to the killing of Black bodies, (b) cause fear of the oppressed to those wielding the power, and (c) decrease the fears of the White populous of the threatening Black man or woman. The dead Black body on display reinforces images of White power. Moreover, the Black body is a form of gratification for necrophiliacs already obsessed with the dehumanization and

27

annihilation of Black citizens. Stated differently, the dead Black body becomes a symbol to soothe White fears and simultaneously a symbol used to invoke fear in Black citizens.

Oxymoronically, necropolitics is interrupted when social justice advocates remind Whites and others that the fear of Black people is a socially constructed political intention that holds no justification and when the images of dead Black bodies are used to expose injustice in the US as opposed to uphold it. In the section below, I discuss how education can be used to interrupt necropolitics and mediate racial oppression.

NECROPOLITICS AND EDUCATION

Throughout the discussion, it has been demonstrated that racial subjugation and class oppression are interconnected and simultaneously shape the lived experiences of young Black men and women, especially those living in high density (urban) communities. The US educational system is a reflection of the White power structure. In brevity, the White dominating class strategically, and systematically, controls major institutions (e.g., public education, housing, medical care) with the intent of protecting their property interests (Ladson-Billings & Tate, 1995). More specifically, Whites have schooling for the continual commodification and exploitation of the Black body and psyche.

Further, I opine that historically the capitalist elite have ghettoized minority schools based on their own racialized beliefs and guaranteed consumption of human labor via the objectification process (Foucault as cited in Rabinow, 1984). I posit that racism is normal and deeply entrenched in the curriculum, schooling practices, discipline policies, and attitudes of teachers in public schools serving our most vulnerable youth. Racism affects relationships, choices, and practices inside and outside of urban school classrooms, and it is recycled and re-consumed in school practices and beliefs recreating a new generation of raced subjects (Goldberg, 1993; Mills, 1997).

Consequently, Black youth are socialized in schools to psychologically embrace White superiority, which eventually leads to physical submission to the White power structure even when it does not further their political or class interests. However, there is evidence too that Blacks have a tradition of utilizing education for personal, community, and racial uplift (Siddle Walker, 2001; Watkins, 2005). Therefore, the task of critical theorists interested in school contexts is to expose racism and describe how it manifests and mutates in classroom discourse and institutional practices.

CRITICALLY ENGAGED EDUCATION

Young people of color deserve schools and teachers that they believe in and who believe in them. They deserve agency over their own lives, opportunities to work to provide for their families, as well as being able to tell their own stories. Creating this would not only be therapeutic for America, it might just be the greatest antiracism work of all time. (J. W. Biehl, high school teacher, Washington, DC, 2015)

I have spent most of my time, efforts, and creativity as a scholar researching and teaching with non-White youth from lower-income and working-class school communities. However, much of my work in university settings is spent teaching to middle-class suburban pre-service teachers and middle-income suburban and rural aspiring school administrators and mentoring racially diverse graduate students interested in critical theories of race and gender in higher education. In reflection, I can state unequivocally that there is a cultural lag between academic theories and on-the-ground work needed in our schools. Nonetheless, I fundamentally believe that education can play a role in helping to alleviate and mediate state sanctioned violence and colonization processes in urban communities.

Our young people (and adult learners) need an education that educates Black children (all children as a matter of fact) from the cradle to the grave about their history and legacy in the world. This type of education serves to instill cultural and racial pride, which ultimately serves to acknowledge Black people's humanity. The world has been taught that Blacks are less than human, are mere chattel, are less intelligent, do not deserve more than a basic education, and are culturally and morally inferior; thus, they should not have the same rights as Whites. Now, students are taught that Blacks do not care about education, lack rationality, and are mentally retarded. Therefore, there is a need for education that counters White supremacist propaganda. It is hard to kill and difficult to allow others to kill when there is respect for one's or a group's contribution to humankind.

Our youth need social media and digital media education that teaches them how not only to be consumers of media, but also producers of media. They can learn to use media to educate themselves, peers, and adults. Also, social media education is needed to learn how to decipher useful information from racist, sexist, homophobic, and xenophobic propaganda. We need to adequately prepare our nation's young citizens to be critical producers, consumers, and disseminators of digitally produced knowledge. If our youth are engaged online, then critically and culturally conscious teachers must be online.

We need efforts to teach youth and adults the reality of racially and politically motivated violence and the historical patterns and processes of colonization in the US and abroad. This history must include state (government nations) sanctioned genocidal violence against the indigenous people of Africa, Australia, Caribbean, Latin America, and islands off the coast of Africa. They must also be deliberately educated on the slave economy of the US, including slave codes, Jim and Jane Crow laws, and the organized assassinations of justice workers, such as Dr. Martin Luther King, Jr., Malcolm X, and Fred Hampton.

We also must teach about the illegal arrests and continued detainment of political activists who spoke out against their government on behalf of Black and Brown people, the poor, and veterans. Along these same lines, our history lessons must teach about the organized political and social efforts of Black men and women and their comrades in the struggle against racial injustice. Specifically, we need to teach the history and practices of organized protests and civil disobedience and the US Constitution and judicial system, which should include voting rights and civil and human rights. The intent is to empower our students and help them develop empathy for victims of violence for too many of our nation's young people are desensitized to violence, due to social media, Hollywood movies, television, and video games. Another objective of these history and contemporary lessons on social justice and judicial activism is to facilitate Black pride and national pride as well as develop a human connection to suffering and resilience.

Of course, we need teachers who are culturally literate and knowledgeable on such topics or are willing to reach out to and partner with other educators or community members who are engaged and aware of efforts to combat racial injustice. All teacher education preparation programs have a responsibility to prepare future educators on democratic education, civic engagement, and culturally responsive practice. *(Re)Teaching Trayvon: Education for racial justice and human freedom* (Evans-Winters & Bethune, 2015) provides a comprehensive historical overview and education manifesto for educators interested in the role of education in interrupting state sanctioned violence against Black men and women, especially our young people.

In the book, alongside discussions on the historical and contemporary context of anti-Black violence, activist scholars put forth methods and strategies to mitigate violence against Black women and men. For example, Brown and Johnson (2015) call for "engaging in a deep and historical examination of the subtext of Black male contempt over time in society and schools" (p. 22). In other words, deeply embedded in the subconscious of our nation is a deep-seated contempt of the Black male body, and this contempt needs to be addressed and interrogated. Contempt leads to suspicion or what Hucks (2015) refers to as *damaging glances*.

Hucks (2015) suggests "moving beyond damaging glances within the context of education will not just uplift students of color, but fully engage those that serve them" (p. 73). Thus, the role of education becomes to provide more positive images of Black people in discourse (e.g., research and policy), social media, and textbooks. Similarly, Kharem and Yearwood (2015), citing the writer/poet/activist James Baldwin and critical educators like Freire (1995), DuBois (1935), Gay (2012), and Gordon (1994), argue for education that "would ensure teachers, administrators, policy makers and the public engage in a critical pedagogy that will eradicate colonial type education predicated upon subservience" (p. 105). In sum, the education system's role is to challenge racial injustice by conscientiously educating teachers and students alike to acknowledge the reality of racial injustice in society, celebrate Black history and humanity across time and space, and teach how to fight against all forms of injustice inside and outside of schools.

CONCLUSION

In conclusion, the White supremacist capitalist patriarchal elite actively engages in a state of perpetual necropolitics among Black individuals and communities. Submission is expected and enacted by exposing citizens to symbolic (visual) and material violence against the Black body. As it has been argued above, over the last few years with the rise of social media, the public has been bombarded by media clips of Black people being assaulted or killed in their own communities with the most emotionally disturbed media images involving the display of young dead bodies. I borrowed from Robert Blauner's (1969) notion of *colonization* and Achille Mbembe's (2003) conceptualization of *necropolitics* to attempt to explain White adult violence against Black civilians.

Throughout the chapter, I argued that White-on-Black violence is intentional, sanctioned, and normalized by policy, institutions (e.g., media, education, religion, judiciary), and the popular imagination. Again, the viewing of the dead body serves to (a) desensitize the populous to the killing of Black bodies, (b) cause fear of the oppressed to those wielding the power, and (c) decrease the fears of the White populous of the threatening Black man or woman. Moreover, the Black body is a form of gratification for necrophiliacs already obsessed with the dehumanization and annihilation of Black citizens. On the other hand, I wholeheartedly believe that schools can mitigate necropolitics.

First, racial justice advocates must remind Whites and others that the fear of Black people is a socially constructed political intention that holds no justification. Images of dead Black bodies are simply evidence of racial injustice in the US. Second, the education system must become a place to facilitate racial, cultural, and national pride for the diverse groups of students it serves—not simply the White middle class. Third, education and racial justice must be connected to larger issues of civil rights and human rights. Black lives matter more, and are more meaningful, when girls and women, the poor and working class, immigrants, undocumented, transgendered, gay and lesbian, disabled, language minorities, Muslims, and native people's lives matter. Consequently, we call for education that serves to further racial justice *and* all aspects of human freedom.

REFERENCES

Alexander, M. (2010). *The new Jim Crow: Mass incarceration in the age of colorblindness.* New York, NY: The New Press.
Anderson, J. D. (1988). *The education of Blacks in the South: 1860–1935.* Chapel Hill, NC: University of North Carolina Press.
Ashkenas, J., & Park, H. (2014). The race gap in America's police departments. *The New York Times.* Retrieved from https://www.nytimes.com/interactive/2014/09/03/us/the-race-gap-in-americas-police-departments.html?_r=0
Augustine, J. (1991). From topos to anthropoid: The city as character in 20th century texts. In M. Caws (Ed.), *City images: Perspectives from literature, philosophy and film* (pp. 73–86). New York, NY: Routledge Press.
Bell, D. (1992). *Faces at the bottom of the well: The permanence of racism.* New York, NY: Basic Books.

Biehl, J. W. (2015). The man in the mirror. In V. Evans-Winters & M. Bethune (Eds.), *(Re)teaching Trayvon: Education for racial justice and human freedom* (pp. 81–94). Rotterdam, The Netherlands: Sense Publishers.

Blauner, R. (1969). Internal colonialism and ghetto revolt. *Social Problems, 16*(4), 393–408.

Brown v. Board of Education. (1954). *Brown v. Board of Education, 347 U.S. 483 (1954) (USSC+).* Retrieved from https://www.ourdocuments.gov/doc.php?flash=true&doc=87&page=transcript

Brown, A. L., & Johnson, M. W. (2015). Blackness enclosed: Understanding the Trayvon Martin incident through the long history of Black male imagery. In V. Evans-Winters & M. Bethune (Eds.), *(Re)teaching Trayvon: Education for racial justice and human freedom* (pp. 11–24). Rotterdam, The Netherlands: Sense Publishers.

Buendía, E. (2011). Reconsidering the urban in urban education: Interdisciplinary conversations. *The Urban Review, 43*(1), 1–21.

Buendía, E., & Ares, N. (2006). *Geographies of difference: The social production of the East Side, West Side, and Central City School.* New York, NY: Peter Lang.

Crenshaw, K., Ocen, P., & Nanda, J. (2015). *Black girls matter: Pushed out, overpoliced and underprotected.* Retrieved from http://www.atlanticphilanthropies.org/app/uploads/2015/09/BlackGirlsMatter_Report.pdf

Delgado, R., & Stefancic, J. (2000). *Critical race theory: The cutting edge* (2nd ed.). Philadelphia, PA: Temple University Press.

Delpit, L. D. (2006). *Other people's children: Cultural conflict in the classroom.* New York, NY: The New Press.

DuBois, W. E. B. (1935). Does the Negro need separate schools? *The Journal of Negro Education, 4*(3), 328–335.

Elias, M. (2013). The school-to-prison pipeline. *Teaching Tolerance, 52*(43), 39–40.

Evans-Winters, V. E., & Bethune, M. C. (Eds.). (2015). *(Re)teaching Trayvon: Education for racial justice and human freedom.* Rotterdam, The Netherlands: Sense Publishers.

Feagin, J. R. (2014). *Racist America: Roots, current realities, and future reparations.* New York, NY: Routledge.

Freire, P. (1995). *The politics of education: Culture power and liberation.* Boston, MA: Bergin & Garvey.

Gay, G. (2012). *Culturally responsive teaching: Theory, research, and practice.* New York, NY: Teachers College Press.

Goldberg, D. T. (1993). *Racist culture: Philosophy and the politics of meaning.* Cambridge, MA: Blackwell Publishers.

Gordon, B. M. (1994). African American cultural knowledge and liberatory education: Dilemmas, problems, and potentials in postmodern American society. In M. J. Shujaa (Ed.), *Too much schooling, too little education: A paradox of Black life in White societies* (pp. 57–78). Trenton, NJ: Africa Third World Press.

Gould, S. J. (1996). *The mismeasure of man.* New York, NY: Norton & Company.

Hoffman, S. (2014). Zero benefit estimating the effect of zero tolerance discipline polices on racial disparities in school discipline. *Educational Policy, 28*(1), 69–95.

Howard, T. C. (2013). How does it feel to be a problem? Black male students, schools, and learning in enhancing the knowledge base to disrupt deficit frameworks. *Review of Research in Education, 37*(1), 54–86.

Hucks, D. C. (2015). Damaging glances in education: Understanding the media's role in stereotype reproduction and reinforcement of negative images of African American males. In V. Evans-Winters & M. Bethune (Eds.), *(Re)teaching Trayvon: Education for racial justice and human freedom* (pp. 65–78). Rotterdam, The Netherlands: Sense Publishers.

Irvine, J. J. (1990). *Black students and school failure: Policies, practices, and prescriptions.* Westport, CT: Greenwood Press.

Katznelson, I. (2005). *When affirmative action was White: An untold history of racial inequality in twentieth-century America.* New York, NY: Norton & Company.

Kharem, H., & Yearwood, T. (2015). No justice in a White man's land: Preparing teachers and teacher educators to erase the mark of inferiority in the wake of Trayvon Martin's death. In V. Evans-Winters & M. Bethune (Eds.), *(Re)teaching Trayvon: Education for racial justice and human freedom* (pp. 95–108). Rotterdam, The Netherlands: Sense Publishers.

Ladson-Billings, G., & Tate, W. F. (1995). Toward a critical race theory of education. *Teachers College Record, 97*(1), 47–68.

Massey, D. S., & Denton, N. A. (1993). *American apartheid: Segregation and the making of the underclass.* Cambridge, MA: Harvard University Press.

Mbembe, A. (2003). Necropolitics. *Public Culture, 15*(1), 11–40.

Mills, C. (1997). *The racial contract.* Ithaca, NY: Cornell University.

Moody, M. (2016). From under-diagnoses to over-representation: Black children, ADHD, and the school-to-prison pipeline. *Journal of African American Studies, 20*(2), 152–163.

Morris, M. W. (2016). *Pushout: The criminalization of Black girls in schools.* New York, NY: The New Press.

National Center for Education Statistics. (2013). *Characteristics of public and private elementary and secondary school teachers in the United States: Results from the 2011–12 schools and staffing survey.* Retrieved from https://nces.ed.gov/fastfacts/display.asp?id=55

New York Civil Liberties Union. (n.d.). *Stop-and-frisk campaign: About the issue.* Retrieved from http://www.nyclu.org/issues/racial-justice/stop-and-frisk-practices

Orfield, G., Kucsera, J., & Siegel-Hawley, G. (2012). E Pluribus … separation: Deepening double segregation for more students. *The Civil Rights Project/Proyecto Derechos Civiles.* Retrieved from http://escholarship.org/uc/item/8g58m2v9#page-2

Potter, G. (1995). The history of policing in the United States. *The Encyclopedia of Police Science.* Retrieved from http://plsonline.eku.edu/sites/plsonline.eku.edu/files/the-history-of-policing-in-us.pdf

Rabinow, P. (1984). *The Foucault reader.* New York, NY: Random House.

Selden, S. (1999). *Inheriting shame: The story of eugenics and racism in America.* New York, NY: Teachers College Press.

Siddle Walker, V. (1996). *Their highest potential: An African American school community in the segregated South.* Chapel Hill, NC: University of North Carolina Press.

Siddle Walker, V. (2001). African American teaching in the South: 1940–1960. *American Educational Research Journal, 38*(4), 751–779.

Smith, P. J. (1998). Our children's burden: The many-headed Hydra of the educational disenfranchisement of Black children. *Howard Law Journal, 42*, 133.

Spring, J. (2016). *Deculturalization and the struggle for equality: A brief history of the education of dominated cultures in the United States* (8th ed.). New York, NY: Routledge.

Stop-and-Frisk Campaign. (n.d.). Retrieved from New York Civil Liberties Union website: http://www.nyclu.org/issues/racial-justice/stop-and-frisk-practices

Sue, D. W., Capodilupo, C. M., Torino, G. C., Bucceri, J. M., Holder, A., Nadal, K. L., & Esquilin, M. (2007). Racial microaggressions in everyday life: Implications for clinical practice. *American psychologist, 62*(4), 271–286.

Trotter, J. W. (1991). *The Great Migration in historical perspective: New dimensions of race, class, and gender.* Bloomington, IN: Indiana University Press.

U.S. Census Bureau. (2015). *Geography: Urban and rural classification.* Retrieved from https://www.census.gov/geo/reference/urban-rural.html

Ward, S. (2004). *Selling places: The marketing and promotion of towns and cities, 1850–2000.* New York, NY: Routledge.

Warren, C. J. E. (1954). Brown v. Board of Education. *United States Reports, 347*(1954), 483.

Watkins, B. (2005). *Black protest thought and education.* New York, NY: Lang.

Wilson, W. J. (1996). *When work disappears: The world of the new urban poor.* Chicago, IL: University of Chicago Press.

Winfield, A. G. (2007). *Eugenics and education in America: Institutionalized racism and the implications of history, ideology, and racism.* New York, NY: Peter Lang.

Woodson, C. G. (1990). *The mis-education of the Negro.* Trenton, NJ: Africa World Press.

Venus E. Evans-Winters
Illinois State University

WAYNE AU

3. WHAT THE RESISTANCE TO HIGH-STAKES TESTING CAN TEACH US ABOUT URBAN CLASSROOMS

High-stakes, standardized testing has become the central tool for education reform over the last several decades, largely based on the premise that such testing holds schools and teachers accountable for educating all children—especially poor children and children of color who are often concentrated in urban school systems (Au, 2016a). As such, high-stakes, standardized testing has been required through federal- and state-level policies, as codified in the Every Student Succeeds Act and its predecessor, No Child Left Behind (Au & Hollar, 2016). However, the over-emphasis on testing has taken its toll on schools and communities (Kamanetz, 2015), where anger among parents, teachers, and students has grown and resulted in organized actions and outright resistance to high-stakes, standardized tests (e.g., Hagopian, 2014a). This rising movement of test resistance can teach us a lot about urban classrooms. In this chapter, I start with an event: the Measure of Academic Progress (MAP) test boycott at Garfield High School in Seattle, Washington. Next, I detail what this event signaled in terms of the national movement against high-stakes standardized testing. I then work through what the test resistance movement teaches us about the issues facing urban classrooms, specifically related to the impact of high-stakes testing and the reasons why such testing will never be able to ameliorate the educational disparities in our cities.

THE EVENT: BOYCOTTING THE MEASURE OF ACADEMIC PROGRESS

In January of 2013, the teachers at Garfield High School in Seattle, Washington held a press conference and informed the world that they would not administer the Measure of Academic Progress (MAP), a district mandated high-stakes, standardized test. And the world responded. Soon, local support grew as the Garfield Parent-Teacher-Student Association (PTSA) officially endorsed the boycott. The Garfield student government leaders vocally supported their teachers. Other schools in the district joined the boycott. Activists in the union, the Seattle Education Association, lent their support. The Seattle NAACP also gave their endorsement (Hagopian, 2014b). Support for the Garfield test boycott also began to flood in from national corners. Teachers in Hawai'i expressed their solidarity. Teachers in Florida had pizza delivered to their colleagues at Garfield High School. Teachers in Berkeley,

G. Sirrakos & C. Emdin (Eds.), Between the World and the Urban Classroom, 35–42.
© *2017 Sense Publishers. All rights reserved.*

Chicago, Portland, and elsewhere took local actions and sent letters of support. Both national teachers' unions sent letters of support to the Garfield teachers (Hagopian, 2014b). Well over 100 scholars from universities around the country signed a petition expressing their solidarity with and support of the Garfield MAP test boycott (Rethinking Schools, 2013).

When test time came, the Garfield PTSA circulated a flyer informing parents of their right to opt out of the MAP testing. In response, dozens of parents sent letters informing the school that they were not allowing their children to take the test. Students also produced and circulated their own flyer telling their peers that they did not have to take the MAP test. On the day of the test, many Garfield students refused to leave their seats, essentially performing an impromptu sit-in by refusing to go to the library to be tested. Other students went to the library but sabotaged the computer-based MAP test by rushing through their answers so fast that the computers automatically registered their exams as invalid (Hagopian, 2014b). The combined resistance of teachers, the student body government, the Black Student Union, parents, scholars from around the country, civil rights leaders, and colleagues from around the city defeated the MAP test at Garfield—which was officially made optional by the Seattle School District for the following academic year.

It is no mistake that the MAP test resistance started at Garfield High School, which historically is at the heart of the African American community in Seattle's urban center. As a school, it has been a hotbed for community resistance and action for decades. For instance, it is the historical home of Seattle's chapter of the Black Panther Party for Self Defense, which focused on providing free breakfast programs and medical care for children, in addition to defending Black people against police violence (Dixon, 2012). Although the Garfield/Seattle MAP test boycott was a singular event, it served as a watershed moment for the national movement against high-stakes, standardized testing, where in the years since we have seen large protests by students in places like Santa Fe, New Mexico and Long Island, New York and massive opt-outs in New York State (200,000 in 2015) and Washington State (over 60,000 in 2015), among others (Foster, 2016; Hagopian, 2015).

However, the nature of test resistance across the country is different depending on race, class, and geography. The test resistance and opt-out movements originating from conservative rural and suburban White communities tend to originate as an expression of fear about the federal government controlling their lives and impeding upon state's rights (Au, 2016b). However, contrary to claims that the test resistance and opt-out movements are only the purview of these White communities (Pondiscio, 2015), students, parents, and communities of color are leading voices in urban test resistance, as we have seen in Chicago, Philadelphia, Seattle, and elsewhere (Hagopian & Network for Public Education, 2015; Rethinking Schools, 2014). As such, the resistance to high-stakes, standardized testing can teach us a lot about the issues facing urban classrooms, particularly because those classrooms feel the effects of such testing more sharply and disproportionately than other classrooms (Au, 2016a).

TESTS ARE CHOKING THE LIFE OUT OF TEACHING AND LEARNING

One of the most pivotal things that the resistance to high-stakes, standardized testing can teach us about urban classrooms is that our nation's obsession with testing is doing damage to our curriculum, teaching, and ultimately our children—particularly in urban schools and communities. Empirical research, both qualitative and quantitative, has consistently shown that high-stakes, standardized testing restricts classroom practices in particular ways, especially since such testing became part of federal education law with the 2002 passing of the No Child Left Behind Act. The tested subjects of English Language Arts and Mathematics become the focus of the curriculum, and teachers shift toward more teacher-centered instruction while shifting away from student-centered construction of knowledge in the classroom (Au, 2007; Center on Education Policy, 2007; Nichols & Berliner, 2007).

Additionally, because these tests concentrate and structure "failure" within low-income communities of color, it is critical to recognize that these negative effects are likewise concentrated in urban classrooms, where nontested subjects like art, music, physical education, science, and social studies are often cut in favor of more focus on test-preparation (Au, 2016a). Further, this concentration of negative effects means that urban classrooms are also more likely to have less engaging teaching and curriculum and less likely to give space, time, and instructional energy toward approaches and content (e.g., multicultural education, Hip Hop pedagogy, ethnic studies, social movements like #BlackLivesMatter, or pressing community concerns such as the Flint water crisis) critical to successfully engaging urban kids in meaningful learning (Emdin, 2016).

As such, high-stakes, standardized testing has bred such robust resistance because it amounts to an attack on effective teaching and learning in urban settings and for children of color. These specific issues highlighted by the movement to resist testing also punctuate an inherent racist and classist inequity: Whiter, more affluent kids in well-resourced suburban schools that traditionally do better on tests and do not face the same pressures are getting a much richer, more balanced, and intellectually more rigorous education than many of their urban, working-class, more diverse peers (Au, 2016a). In this way, the disparate impacts of high-stakes standardized testing on urban classrooms also teach us that systemic racism and inequality persist through our systems of testing and education.

SYSTEMIC INEQUALITIES ARE ALIVE AND WELL IN OUR SCHOOLS

Advocates for the use of high-stakes, standardized testing often argue that such tests allow authorities to hold schools and teachers accountable for the education of working-class Black and Brown children in urban classrooms, often as an expression of civil rights (Au, 2016a). These arguments are belied by the fact that a decade and a half of federally mandated high-stakes testing has not created educational equality or closed any test-based achievement gaps (National Research

Council, 2011; Ravitch, 2013), and they are belied by the above-mentioned disparate impacts on children of color. The resistance to high-stakes, standardized testing not only teaches us about these realities, it also highlights how these tests have never been about educational equity for urban classrooms, historically or conceptually.

Historically, our entire system of standardized testing (as well as systems of educational tracking) has its roots in early intelligence testing by prominent U.S. psychologists, like Lewis Terman, in the early 1900s. These psychologists gave what they claimed were "objective" intelligence tests to masses of WWI U.S. Army recruits, finding that the poor were less intelligent than the rich; immigrants were less intelligent than those born in the US; and that African Americans, Native Americans, and Mexican Americans were less intelligent than Whites, among other racist claims used to support the growing eugenics movement at the time (Blanton, 2003; Gould, 1996). Under the leadership of these same psychologists, similar tests were adopted en masse in major urban school systems to provide a supposedly "objective" way of classifying and sorting the large numbers of children entering into the public school system at the time (Au, 2009; Chapman, 1988).

While it is easy to relegate racist notions of intelligence and faulty notions of objectivity as being in the past, these ghosts still haunt urban classrooms today in both blatant and commonsense ways. Herrnstein and Murray's (1996) *The Bell Curve* and Rushton and Jensen's (2005) research explicitly relied on blatantly racist notions of intelligence. Further, our current high-stakes, standardized tests rest on the assumption that they provide objective and accurate measures of teaching and learning, a commonsense view that is held despite the fact that our contemporary tests essentially produce the same race, wealth, and language gaps as the blatantly racist standardized tests of 100 years ago (Au, 2009). Thus, based on false notions of racist objectivity and dressed in the myth of meritocracy that denies the existence of structural inequalities, such testing has functioned as a modern tool for both categorizing urban students and justifying the unequal outcomes the tests produce (Au, 2016a).

The resistance to high-stakes tests also teaches us other ways such testing is fundamentally not designed to support equity in urban classrooms. For instance, the persistently low test scores associated with urban schools and communities (Ladson-Billings, 2006) have, for decades, most strongly correlated with socioeconomic resources outside of and around schools. As Berliner (2013) explains:

> Virtually every scholar of teaching and schooling knows that … school effects account for about 20% of the variation in achievement test scores…. On the other hand, out-of-school variables account for about 60% of the variance that can be accounted for in student achievement. In aggregate, such factors as family income; the neighborhood's sense of collective efficacy, violence rate, and average income; medical and dental care available and used; level of food insecurity; number of moves a family makes over the course of a

child's school years; ... provision of high-quality early education in the neighborhood; language spoken at home; and so forth, all substantially affect school achievement. (para. 13–14)

As the test resistance movement has taught us, teachers and schools are critically necessary in education, but they alone are insufficient for providing a quality education for urban classrooms. Structural access to resources outside of school are the most important factors in the educational success of children, such that attempts to create greater educational equity sans addressing these greater racial and socioeconomic inequalities will inherently have limited effect.

Indeed, the above point highlights how the resistance to high-stakes testing teaches us yet another lesson about systemic inequalities in urban classrooms: Standardized tests like the ones given in schools today are not designed for all kids to succeed, and instead actually require certain numbers of children to fail. Whether it is a norm-referenced test or the scaled scores generated from a criterion reference test (Popham, 2001; Tan & Michel, 2011), high-stakes, standardized tests are constructed such that scores are distributed on a "normal" bell curve, with some children scoring high, a lot of children scoring in the middle, and some children scoring low on the test (Weber, 2015b). The issue is that, as Berliner's (2013) above point suggests, the distribution of scores along the "normal" bell curve correlates most strongly with the students' socioeconomic status (Weber, 2015a). Additionally, it is important to point out that failure on these tests (which are constructed to create levels of failure) has real consequences because research has indicated that having a high-stakes test as a high school exit exam can result in a 12.5% increase in the likelihood of young people getting incarcerated, as test failure cuts off many opportunities outside of and after school (Baker & Lang, 2013). Given that people of color in the United States are disproportionately poor, that there are high concentrations of poverty in many urban centers (Fabricant & Fine, 2013), and that test-defined failure gets concentrated in low-income communities of color putting them at the most risk of test-related, adverse consequences, the resistance to high-stakes testing continues to teach us about how urban classrooms are subject to ongoing and systemic racist and socioeconomic inequalities. However, as we know from history, urban communities have always fought such injustices.

URBAN SCHOOLS AND COMMUNITIES WILL FIGHT FOR EDUCATIONAL JUSTICE

The final and perhaps most important lesson that the resistance to high-stakes, standardized testing can teach us about urban classrooms is that urban students, parents, teachers, and community members will fight for educational justice through powerful activism and action. At the start of this chapter, I relayed the story of the teacher boycott of the MAP test in Seattle, Washington, which with its student and community support highlights that students and teachers in urban classrooms can and will resist unjust policies and practices (Hagopian, 2014b). However, there are many more examples of urban communities organizing against such testing. In Providence, Rhode Island, students in the Providence Student Union walked the streets dressed as zombies to illustrate how high-stakes testing was killing their education and numbing their minds (McKay, Regunberg, & Shea, 2014). In Portland, Oregon, the Portland Student Union organized a successful student walkout after struggling with the district over the improper use of high-stakes tests in their schools (Garcia, 2014). New York City parent and public school teacher, Jia Lee, tells the story of how she organized with her community at the Salt of the Earth School to lead an opt-out movement and make a public protest to the NYC schools chancellor, a protest which spread to other schools like the Brooklyn New School (Hagopian, 2014c). Teacher Sarah Chambers (2014) relays the story of how she and her colleagues at Saucedo Academy in southwest Chicago led a successful boycott of their state exam, the ISAT. Also in Chicago, parents held a "play-in" at the Chicago Public Schools headquarters, where they and their children settled down in the Chicago Public Schools lobby to play in protest of how high-stakes testing was taking play and recess out of the earlier grades and negatively impacting their children's education (Roberts, 2014). Dao Tran (2014), a parent at Castle Bridge School in New York City, helped organize a successful high-stakes test opt out and boycott movement at her school. These examples show that despite the media's and politicians' insistence that test resistance is mainly a White rural and suburban phenomenon (Pondiscio, 2015), urban students and communities are in fact leading profound resistance movements in their cities. However, unlike their White counterparts, urban education activists center their test resistance around a politics of educational justice and the racism embedded in and attached to high-stakes, standardized testing.

CONCLUSION

There is so much happening right now in the world that can teach us about urban classrooms, and in many ways high-stakes, standardized testing are ideal for getting at those issues since so many of our educational policies are explicitly aimed at "fixing" urban education. Within the critiques of testing, we see the kernels of what is necessary to fix our urban education systems: attention to urban infrastructure, including affordable housing, livable wages, healthcare, affordable childcare for working families, and quality early childhood education. These critiques that drive the testing resistance movement also teach us that urban communities demand to be heard and included in the education of their children, and they do not appreciate these policies and practices that come down from powers that be, sitting on high somewhere distant from their kids and their classrooms. Finally, and perhaps most importantly, contrary to stereotypes so often trotted out by the media, politicians, and even some academics, urban communities care deeply about the quality of education for their children and they are willing to fight for it when pushed.

REFERENCES

Au, W. (2007). High-stakes testing and curricular control: A qualitative metasynthesis. *Educational Researcher, 36*(5), 258–267.

Au, W. (2009). *Unequal by design: High-stakes testing and the standardization of inequality.* New York, NY: Routledge.

Au, W. (2016a). Meritocracy 2.0: High-stakes, standardized testing as a racial project of neoliberal multiculturalism. *Educational Policy, 30*(1), 39–62. Retrieved from http://doi.org/10.1177/0895904815614916

Au, W. (2016b). Techies, the tea party, and the common core: The rise of the new upper middle class and tensions in the rightist politics of federal education reform. *The Educational Forum, 80*(2), 208–224. Retrieved from http://doi.org/10.1080/00131725.2016.1135378

Au, W., & Hollar, J. (2016). Opting out of the education reform industry. *Monthly Review, 67*(10), 29–37.

Baker, O., & Lang, K. (2013, June). *The effect of high school exit exams on graduation, employment, wages and incarceration* (Working Paper No. 19182). Cambridge, MA: National Bureau of Economic Research.

Berliner, D. C. (2013). Effects of inequality and poverty vs. teachers and schooling on America's youth. *Teachers College Record, 115*(12). Retrieved from http://www.tcrecord.org/Content.asp?ContentId=16889

Blanton, C. K. (2003). From intellectual deficiency to cultural deficiency. *Pacific Historical Review, 72*(1), 39–62.

Center on Education Policy. (2007). *Choices, changes, and challenges: Curriculum and instruction in the NCLB era.* Washington, DC: Author. Retrieved from http://www.cep-dc.org/displayDocument.cfm?DocumentID=312

Chambers, S. (2014). Ice the ISAT: Boycotting the test under Mayor Rahm Emanuel's regime. In J. Hagopian (Ed.), *More than a score: The new uprising against high-stakes testing* (pp. 113–122). Chicago, IL: Haymarket Books.

Chapman, P. D. (1988). *Schools as sorters: Lewis M. Terman, applied psychology, and the intelligence testing movement, 1890–1930.* New York, NY: New York University Press.

Dixon, A. (2012). *My people are rising: Memoir of a Black Panther Party captain.* Chicago, IL: Haymarket Books.

Emdin, C. (2016). *For White folks who teach in the hood ... and the rest of y'all too: Reality pedagogy and urban education.* Boston, MA: Beacon Press.

Fabricant, M., & Fine, M. (2013). *The changing politics of education: Privatization and the dispossessed lives left behind.* Boulder, CO: Paradigm Publishers.

Foster, J. B. (2016). The opt out revolt: Democracy and education. *Monthly Review, 67*(10). Retrieved from http://monthlyreview.org/2016/03/01/the-opt-out-revolt/

Garcia, A. (2014). Walk out! In J. Hagopian (Ed.), *More than a score: The new uprising against high-stakes testing* (pp. 147–160). Chicago, IL: Haymarket Books.

Gould, S. J. (1996). *The mismeasure of man* (Rev. and expanded.). New York, NY: Norton.

Hagopian, J. (Ed.). (2014a). *More than a score: The new uprising against high-stakes testing.* Chicago, IL: Haymarket Books.

Hagopian, J. (2014b). Our destination is not on the MAP. In J. Hagopian (Ed.), *More than a score: The new uprising against high-stakes testing* (pp. 31–47). Chicago, IL: Haymarket Books.

Hagopian, J. (2014c). Salt of the earth school: "They can't break us." Interview with Jia Lee. In J. Hagopian (Ed.), *More than a score: The new uprising against high-stakes testing* (pp. 107–112). Chicago, IL: Haymarket Books.

Hagopian, J. (2015, October 30). *Obama regrets "taking the joy out of teaching and learning" with too much testing.* Retrieved from http://www.commondreams.org/views/2015/10/30/obama-regrets-taking-joy-out-teaching-and-learning-too-much-testing

Hagopian, J., & Network for Public Education. (2015, May 5). *Resistance to high stakes tests serves the cause of equity in education: A reply to "we oppose anti-testing efforts."* Retrieved from http://www.networkforpubliceducation.org/2015/05/resistance-to-high-stakes-tests-serves-the-cause-of-equity-in-education/

Herrnstein, R. J., & Murray, C. A. (1996). *The bell curve: Intelligence and class structure in American life*. New York, NY: Free Press Paperbacks.

Kamanetz, A. (2015). *The test: Why our schools are obsessed with standardized testing – but you don't have to be*. New York, NY: Public Affairs.

Ladson-Billings, G. (2006). From the achievement gap to the education debt: Understanding achievement in U.S. schools. *Educational Researcher, 35*(7), 3–12.

McKay, C., Regunberg, A., & Shea, T. (2014). Testing assumptions: Zombies, flunkies, and the providence student union. In J. Hagopian (Ed.), *More than a score: The new uprising against high-stakes testing* (pp. 135–140). Chicago, IL: Haymarket Books.

National Research Council. (2011). *Incentives and test-based accountability in education*. Washington, DC: National Academies Press.

Nichols, S. L., & Berliner, D. C. (2007). *Collateral damage: How high-stakes testing corrupts America's schools*. Cambridge, MA: Harvard Education Press.

Pondiscio, R. (2015, March 25). *Opting out, race, and reform*. Retrieved from https://edexcellence.net/articles/opting-out-race-and-reform

Popham, W. J. (2001). *The truth about testing: An educator's call to action*. Alexandria, VA: Association for Supervision and Curriculum Development.

Ravitch, D. (2013). *Reign of error: The hoax of the privatization movement and the danger to America's public schools*. New York, NY: Alfred A. Knopf.

Rethinking Schools. (2013, January 21). *Leading educators support teacher test boycott*. Retrieved from https://rethinkingschoolsblog.wordpress.com/2013/01/21/leading-educators-support-teacher-test-boycott/

Rethinking Schools. (2014). The gathering resistance to standardized tests. *Rethinking Schools, 28*(3). Retrieved from http://www.rethinkingschools.org/archive/28_03/edit2283.shtml

Roberts, K. (2014). Playing for the schools we want. In J. Hagopian (Ed.), *More than a score: The new uprising against high-stakes testing* (pp. 205–210). Chicago, IL: Haymarket Books.

Rushton, P. J., & Jensen, A. R. (2005). Thirty years of research on race differences in cognitive ability. *Psychology, Public Policy, and Law, 11*(2), 234–294.

Tan, X., & Michel, R. (2011). *Why do standardized testing programs report scaled scores?: Why not just report the raw or percent-correct scores?* Retrieved from https://www.ets.org/Media/Research/pdf/RD_Connections16.pdf

Tran, D. X. (2014). Forget teaching to the test–Castle Bridge boycotts it! In J. Hagopian (Ed.), *More than a score: The new uprising against high-stakes testing* (pp. 211–218). Chicago, IL: Haymarket Books.

Weber, M. (2015a, May 24). *Standardized tests: Symptoms, not causes*. Retrieved from http://jerseyjazzman.blogspot.com/2015/05/standardized-tests-symptoms-not-causes.html

Weber, M. (2015b, September 25). *Common core testing: Who's the real "liar"?* Retrieved from http://jerseyjazzman.blogspot.com/2015/09/common-core-testing-whos-real-liar.html

Wayne Au
University of Washington Bothell

TREVA B. LINDSEY

4. WHY YOU SO ANGRY?

Serena Williams, Black Girl Pain, and the
Pernicious Power of Stereotypes

In late Summer 2015, the world tuned in to watch Serena Williams make herstory at the U.S. Open. With the possibilities of tying Steffi Graf's record of winning 22 Grand Slam Singles titles and being only the fourth woman in history to achieve a calendar year Grand Slam, the fervor around Williams reached a fever pitch as she walked onto the court of the semifinals in Flushing, New York. Having already solidified a legacy as one of the best athletes of all time, a victory at the 2015 U.S. Open would further strengthen the convincing argument that Williams is the best female tennis player of all time. For many, a victory in the semifinals felt like a sure thing, especially after her victory over her sister Venus Williams in the quarterfinals. Fans prepared for what they thought would be an inevitable appearance in the U.S. Open finals. Throughout the 2015 Grand Slam season, Serena Williams played some of her best tennis in her storied career. Consequently, her loss to Roberta Vinci, a comparatively lesser-known player, in the semifinals shocked viewers and fans. Although her dominance in women's tennis remained indisputable, this particular and unexpected loss provided detractors with fodder for discrediting her tremendous career and for revisiting longstanding criticisms of Williams's on and off the court behavior.

Williams's career is marked by the juxtaposition of the significant adoration of her fans and the pervasive disdain of her critics. To many, she is the barrier breaking, athletic phenomenon who, along with her sister, popularized women's tennis in the modern era and changed the way women can and do play the sport (Araton, 2015). To others, she is an inconsistent, aggressive, overrated diva (O'Shea, 2010). These starkly oppositional views of Williams capture the polarizing ways her image circulates in mass media. Her body, attitude, style of play, and career choices and trajectory situate her at the nexus of celebrity, surveillance, scrutiny, and adulation. The frequency with which her body and her attitude arise in conversations about her greatness or lack thereof mirror a distinct history of Black women's bodies and their bodies of work being engaged within popular culture. Although not all critiques of Williams traffic in historical discourses about Black womanhood, the pervasiveness of racial and gender stereotypes and racially coded language embedded in discussions about Serena Williams connect to a larger history of racism and sexism targeting Black women and girls.

G. Sirrakos & C. Emdin (Eds.), Between the World and the Urban Classroom, 43–52.

This chapter critically considers how racial and gender stereotypes inscribe conversations about Serena Williams. Using Williams as a primary subject and "site" of inquiry, I explore how longstanding stereotypes about Black women continue to affect how people engage Black women and girls. While Williams is exceptional in her status as a successful professional athlete and as a well-known celebrity, her encounters with racism and sexism do not deviate from a history of Black women being devalued or rendered "spectacle" through racial and gender stereotypes (Harris-Perry, 2011). These stereotypes permeate the celebrity sports culture Williams inhabits as well as the daily experiences of Black women and girls. From the televised tennis courts Williams dominates to the urban, public school classrooms Black girls populate, the prevalence of racial and gender stereotypes impacts how we view, interpret, and criticize Black women and girls' behavior as deviant, disruptive, and unruly. Figurations of Black women and girls as a "problem" can be found in sports writing about Serena Williams and in teacher reports about Black girls "misbehaving" in class.

Ruth Nicole Brown, a pioneering scholar of Black girlhood studies, states that "if you are privileged to be in consistent relationship with Black girls and research on Black girlhood, then you will be immediately dissatisfied by literature that frames being Black and female as the problem" (Brown, 2013, p. 8). Moving beyond Black girls and women as "problems" requires an unpacking of stereotypes about their bodies and dispositions (Brown, 2013). This does not mean stepping away from addressing the numerous problems Black women and girls face, but shifting our focus from seeing Black women and girls as "problems" to comprehending problematic systems disproportionately affecting Black girls and women. It is a call to uncover the myriad ways in which racial and gender stereotypes contribute to discourses of Black woman/girl pathology and to policies and regulations that unjustly target Black women and girls. Brown asserts that we must hear Black girl truths. Brown alongside other scholars, such as Bettina Love, Elaine Richardson, bell hooks, Monique Morris, and Aimee Meredith Cox, opened the field of Black girlhood studies to comprehensively understand challenges to and possibilities for the cultivation of Black girl genius. Rather than discourses of blame and shame, Black girlhood studies scholars offer discussions of systemic disparities and perpetual inequality as well as Black girls thriving.

Racial and gender stereotypes embed themselves within systems and institutions. From Black girls in Detroit to a Black woman striving for her 23rd Grand Slam singles title, the impact of racial and gender stereotypes reverberates on multiple frequencies in Black girls' and women's lives. At the intersection of being Black- and woman-identified are as Melissa Harris-Perry (2011) identifies, "derogatory assumptions" about Black women's "character and identity" (p. 5). Furthermore, Harris-Perry argues that, "these assumptions shape the social world that Black women must accommodate or resist" (p. 5). For critics of Williams, racial and gender stereotypes validate intense scrutiny of her body, her style of play, her off-court activities, and her personality. For school administrators and teachers, these same stereotypes reinforce racially-disparate disciplining of Black girls (Morris, 2016) and misrecognition of Black girls' behaviors and attitudes (Craven, 2015).

If one of the most well-known and lauded Black women in the world cannot escape the perniciousness of racial and gender stereotypes, how can we reasonably expect Black girls to thrive in spaces where these stereotypes influence the practices of those charged with educating, caring for, and protecting them? Serena Williams is not more important than any other Black girl, woman, or woman-identified person, but her story as it pertains to racial and gender stereotypes is instructive for more fully grasping how and why Black girls and women become viewed and treated as "problems." Williams's unquestionable excellence in her field does not release her from the burden of racial and gender stereotypes. Notably, her heightened visibility uniquely situates her as a subject through which we can explore how and why stereotypes of Black womanhood and girlhood continue to shape the lives of Black women and girls. More specifically, we can reckon with how these stereotypes contribute to racial and gender disparities extant in education.

#ASSAULTATSPRINGVALLEYHIGH: BLACK GIRL PAIN

On Monday, October 26, 2015, a 16-year-old Black female student was "placed in a chokehold, flipped over in her seat, then dragged and thrown across her classroom before being handcuffed by a South Carolina school officer" (Craven, 2015, para. 1). Video footage of the violent encounter went viral within 24 hours. #AssaultAtSpringValleyHigh trended on Twitter as people posted the video and debated the actions of Richland County Senior Deputy Ben Fields. As people pondered what actions might justify the violence Officer Fields enacted on the Black girl in the video, few appeared to question the very presence of a senior deputy in a high school. How does an alleged classroom disruption lead to a trained school resource officer placing a teenager in a chokehold?

Within moments of Officer Fields's arrival, the young girl is physically assaulted. Reports indicate that a teacher called for an officer after the student victim refused to stop using her cell phone during a math class or to leave after being asked to do so by the teacher (Golding, 2015). Although conflicting reports surfaced regarding whether the student became physically confrontational with the officer at any point during the assault (Yan, 2015), available videos of the violent incident irrefutably show a disturbing escalation of violence directed at a 16-year-old student who at worse refused to get off her cell phone and attempted to defend herself against an officer physically attacking her.

The viral video raised and should raise important questions about the actions of the officer as well as the utility of policing in schools. The kind of violence seen in the #AssaultAtSpringValleyHigh video should spark concerns about how schools treat racial and ethnic minority students. What acts of "disruption," if any, warrant physical disciplining by a police officer? How does the presence of police shift how schools think about responding to violations of established student codes of conduct?

If policies exist that frame students as criminals, how can school officers be seen as viable figures committed to the *protection* of their students?

Another important aspect of this case was the framing of the student victim as "disruptive." After the video went viral, details about the young victim's life surfaced. She had recently lost her mother, became an orphan, and started living in foster care (Roberston, 2015). Coupled with the assault and the incessant replaying of the video after it went viral, it is difficult to imagine this girl not being emotionally devastated. As she entered into the classroom on that Monday, she traveled with grief, loss, and uncertainty. Her pain seemed illegible to her teacher and to Officer Fields. She was marked as "disruptive" and as a "problem." Her emotional well-being, particularly as it pertained to a devastating set of circumstances beyond her control, did not factor into how school officials handled her. Her pain was misrecognized as deviance, willful defiance, and bad behavior. The teacher, the officer, and the educational system failed to recognize that her behavior was rooted in a real and lived pain. No one accounted for the reality of her Black girl pain when the teacher and the officer marked her as a "problem."

On September 14, 2003, the older sister of Venus and Serena Williams, Yetunde Price, was shot and killed in a drive-by in Compton, California. After the death of their sister, the Williams family released the following statement:

> We are extremely shocked, saddened, and devastated by the shooting death of our beloved Yetunde. She was our nucleus and our rock. She was our personal assistant, confidant, and advisor to her sisters, and her death leaves a void that can never be filled. (Faussett, Dillman, & Glover, 2003, para. 4)

This public statement of grief and sadness, however, did not stop the media from harshly criticizing both Williams sisters in the months after the murder of Yetunde. Within a few months, commentators began framing the absence of the sisters from major tournaments as evidence of the sisters' self-centeredness and of the "allure" of this dynamic duo waning (Wertheim, 2004). After 8 months away from competing in tournaments, Serena Williams returned to the world of tennis at the Nasdaq 100 tournament in Miami. She won. Despite her victory, commentators and critics returned to her absence for several months and depicted it as self-serving. Critics used her appearances at nontennis events and her endorsements to substantiate their claims about her as disrespectful and brazen. Whereas Williams's interviews during this period gestured toward the death of her sister causing her to restructure her priorities as represented in statements such as the following: "Tennis was just so much of my life, and then you begin to realize there are just so many things in life that are more important than hitting the ball over the net" (Schelzig, 2004, para. 11). Few media outlets or critics created space for Serena to mourn and grieve.

Delia Douglas (2012) argues, "Mainstream media narratives did not regard the murder of Yetunde as a factor in either the sisters' absence or their performance on the tour in 2004" (pp. 137–138). The trauma inflicted upon Serena by the murder of her sister was invisible to media and critics. They viewed her as an overpaid celebrity not producing at the level consumers expected, as a human commodity. The lack of recognition of her trauma gave the false appearance that Serena should be impervious to pain. In contrast, her White counterparts were not subject to such misconceptions. Serena was expected to perform, without consideration of her unique and painful circumstances. Consciously and unconsciously the media and her critics demanded that she embody the long-standing myth of the "strongblackwoman" (Harris-Lacewell, 2001).

Despite the potential and actuality of the strongblackwoman myth/stereotype serving as Harris-Perry (2011) identifies, "a constructive role model," the danger of the myth is framing Black women and girls as "super-strong." Possessing super-strength is not in and of itself damaging, but the positioning of Black women and girls as non- and or super-human as it pertains to their emotional well-being contributes to an erasure of the fullness of Black women's and girls' humanity. If prevailing narratives posit Black women as unwaveringly resilient and perpetually tenacious, where is there space to reckon with their pain, vulnerability, fears, and insecurities? Expectations for emotional stability and maturity in the face of trauma or formidable challenges can imprison Black women and girls.

The racial/gender stereotype of the strongblackwoman results in the figuration of Black women as uniquely able to bear the unbearable. While resiliency is a quality most would applaud, the myth of Black women having untiring strength to endure horrific circumstances leaves Black female-identified people with the unjust burden of being impervious. According to psychologist Regina Romero (2000), "Society expects the African American woman to handle losses, traumas, failed relationships, and the dual oppressions of racism and sexism" (p. 227). Beyond a societal investment in the strongblackwoman myth, the internalization of this myth can cause irreparable harm to the physical and mental health of Black women and girls (Romero, 2000). In addition to wrestling with challenges, Black women and girls may feel inadequate because they cannot "overcome." They could also encounter harsh criticism for not living up to this problematic ideal.

Important connections exist between the #AssaultAtSpringValleyHigh and Serena Williams's experiences during the 2004 tennis season. The pain of both of these Black female-identified persons was only cursorily addressed. Whereas mass media did not center Serena's pain, the teacher and the school resource officer at Spring Valley High School responded to this Black girl without consideration of her pain. The way the school resource officer threw her out of the chair and across the room was appalling. The debate between those appalled and those defending the officer's violent actions, however, revealed a troubling fault line in how institutions perceive and respond to Black girl pain. Although few news outlets reported about the death of the girl's mother, conversations about what circumstances would justify the officer physically assaulting this student reached a fever pitch as the video went viral. The search for a justification indicated that to some, a set of behaviors existed to validate the vicious and violent treatment of a student. Finding out that she posed no physical threat to either her teacher or her fellow students did not deter people from speculating about the "threat" she posed by being unresponsive.

Although the #AssaultAtSpringValleyHigh represents a more extreme form of violence against Black girls in classrooms, unruliness of Black girls' bodies in classrooms often results in harsher disciplinary actions from teachers and school administrators (Crenshaw, Ocen, & Nanda, 2015). In Monique Morris's (2016) groundbreaking book, *Pushout: The Criminalization of Black Girls in Schools*, Morris documents and analyzes the ways in which schools treat Black girls as criminals. Startling statistics, such as Black girls comprise more than a third of all school arrests while only representing 16% of female students, help substantiate Morris's argument that, "the pushout of Black girls—the collection of policies, practices, and consciousness that fosters their invisibility, marginalizes their pain and opportunities, and facilitates their criminalization—goes unchallenged" (p. 24). The 16-year-old violently assaulted at Spring Valley High School experienced both the criminalization of her "unruly" behavior and the systemic marginalization of her pain. She was arrested after being assaulted, and the video of her assault was inescapable of social media.

Compassionate curiosity about her alleged refusal to comply with the teacher or the school resource officer did not spark a broader conversation about how to deal with Black girl pain in humane and productive ways in classrooms. The student's victimization resonated within a broader context of Black girl pain being illegible. The ideal of the strongblackwoman is more permanently fixed in the general consciousness, and therefore, despite her mental or emotional health, school officials expected her to perform as though unaffected by a devastating set of circumstances. Too often people read Black girls' pain as disruptive and unproductive. Similar to the media's criticisms of Serena Williams in 2004, school officials interpreted the actions of the teenager assaulted at Spring Valley High School as "bad behavior." Without consideration of the unique conditions under which this young girl and Williams were being asked to perform, responses to their "misbehavior" were swift and harsh.

The pernicious combination of racism, sexism, and in many cases poverty, affect how Black girls experience the world and how non-Black girls respond to Black girls experiencing the world. One of the main, although understudied ways in which schools engage with Black girls is through implicit bias. The Kirwan Institute (2016) defines implicit bias as,

> The attitudes or stereotypes that affect our understanding, actions, and decisions in an unconscious manner. These biases, which encompass both favorable and unfavorable assessments, are activated involuntarily and without an individual's awareness or intentional control. Residing deep in the subconscious, these biases are different from known biases that individuals may choose to conceal for the purposes of social and/or political correctness. Rather, implicit biases are not accessible through introspection. (para. 1)

For Black girls in schools, implicit bias often results in differential treatment and expectations in classrooms. Monique Morris (2016) argues that, "a teacher may believe he or she treats all students the same even while aspects of their engagement are reflecting latent biases" (p. 51). Whereas implicit bias arguably sounds less negative and more "interpersonal" in praxis, it contributes to systemic criminalization and devaluation of Black girls in classrooms. Bias relies upon deeply entrenched racial, gender, and class stereotypes about Black women and girls. Sexuality, ability, ethnicity, religion, and language also contribute to stereotyping of Black girls in specific and interconnected ways. Frequently, Black girls live at the intersection of multiple identity-based stereotypes.

In 1988, Black feminist scholar Deborah King conceptualized *multiple jeopardy* as a lens through which people could unpack the historical and lived experiences of Black women. Multiple jeopardy, as King asserts, "refers not only to several simultaneous oppressions, but to the multiplicative relationships among them as well" (p. 47). Stereotyping of Black girls occurs at the site of collision among race, gender, class, sexuality, ethnicity, ability, language, religion, and other social identifiers. Black girls in classrooms knowingly and unknowingly confront the consequences of racist, sexist, classist, homophobic, transphobic, Islamophobic, ableist, and antiimmigrant stereotypes from teachers, administrators, counselors, coaches, school personnel, and fellow students. Stereotypes about the loudness, superhuman strength, bad attitudes, uncontrollable anger, and hypersexuality of Black women and girls influence how schools educate, discipline, and imagine possibility for girls like the Spring Valley High School victim.

Stereotypes about Black girls derive from and help to perpetuate racist and sexist ideologies. Stereotypes are foundational to what Patricia Hill Collins (1998) theorized as controlling images of Black womanhood. Specifically, "certain assumed qualities that are attached to Black women are used to justify oppression" (p. 7). Stereotypes and controlling images embolden discriminatory social practices against Black women and girls, particularly in institutional settings such as schools. School professionals may actively rail against stereotypes about Black girls while simultaneously engaging in practices and behaviors that perpetuate discrimination against and disparate treatment of Black girls. Stereotypes tend to function as unstated "institutional truths," which dictate policies, rules, and codes of conduct.

YOU MAD HUH?: THE DETRIMENTAL EFFECTS OF THE "ANGRYBLACKWOMAN" STEREOTYPE

Stereotypes alongside controlling images also produce falsehoods about Black girls in classrooms. Whereas the "strongblackwoman" myth rendered the Spring Valley High School victim's pain illegible and unaccounted for, the stereotype of the "angryblackwoman" compounded the abhorrent mishandling of her "disruptive behavior." Historically and contemporarily, loudness and assertiveness equate with unruliness and aggressiveness when applied to Black female-identified bodies. Anger, whether warranted or not, is inextricably linked to understandings of Black women's and girls' personalities (Childs, 2005). Despite studies proving that, "young black women are not more prone to angry outbursts or violent behavior" (Sargent, 2016, para. 5), Black women's and girls' reactions to contentious or difficult situations are often read as "angry" and "unproductive."

In a 2015 *USA Today* article, the headline stated, "Angry Serena Williams Taunts Wimbledon Crowd: 'Don't Try Me.'" The article details a "history" of Williams's responses to tense situations between her and umpires and crowds throughout her trailblazing career. From quips such as, "Serena wouldn't be Serena if she didn't give just a little attitude" (Chase, 2016, para. 2), to a brief recollection of Williams's confrontations with chair umpires and hostile crowds, the article appeared to celebrate her newfound "equanimity," while still framing her as "angry." The fact the headline used "angry" as a modifier for Williams is important to note. The article provides little to no context for Williams's perceived anger. They do not characterize her as frustrated or the crowd as combative—she alone bears the burden of emotionality. Framing her as angry also delegitimizes her as a competitor. The article leads with her anger. The title and subsequent article pander to a troubling history of mischaracterizing and oversimplifying the emotional subjectivities of Black women and girls.

Widely accepted narratives about Serena Williams's lack of sportsmanship dovetail from perceptions of her being angry ("Unsportsmanlike Conduct," 2016). Her loudness, both in physical presentation (colorful ensembles and hairstyles honed within Black communities) and sonic presence (sounds she makes while playing), render her deviant from and disruptive of the status quo in women's tennis. When she reacts to bad calls, comments/slurs from the crowd, or internal frustration about her level of play, these reactions become fodder for a historically-rooted discourse about Black women being irrationally and unjustly angry. Devoid of any context of the numerous reasons a Black woman could or should be angry, the labeling of Black women as "always angry" provides justifications for harsher penalties for those transgressing established notions of rational emotionality.

Anger is not simply assigned to "loud" Black women and girls. The Spring Valley High School victim's silence and alleged verbal refusal to not comply with her teacher's rule intimated irrational anger for many on social media responding to the video of the assault. Critics of the victim framed her quietness as an act of anger and willful deviance. She may have been angry about the loss of her mother or recently being placed in foster care, but the stereotype of angryblackwoman flattened how the school and many online spectators responded to her actions. She was a problem that needed to be fixed. Serena, in order to be a true champion, had to relinquish anger. Whether in professional sports or in classrooms, the demand for Black women to not be angry coincides with the overarching expectation that Black women and girls are angrier than other race/gender groups.

A 2009 study conducted by J. Celeste Walley-Jean found that young African American women reported a greater tendency to experience and suppress intense angry feelings rather than expressing them either physically or verbally. The study also concluded that, "Black women reported significantly less frequent angry feelings in situations where they may receive criticism, perceived disrespect and negative evaluations (i.e. angry reaction)" (as cited in Sargent, 2016, para. 5). This study debunks the angryblackwoman myth, and yet this myth remains prevalent in both popular culture and in the subtext of disciplinary outcomes for school-age Black girls. This stereotype plays an integral role in the racially disparate suspension and expulsion rates for African American girls. The cost of Black women's and girls' perceived anger exists in the form of heightened media scrutiny and professional discrediting as well as in teachers' willingness to remove Black girls from their classrooms, both temporarily and permanently. Black women and girls bear the undue burdens of suppressing their emotions in tense situations and combatting a stereotype that can negatively affect their educational and professional opportunities.

CONCLUSION

Both the #AssaultAtSpringValleyHigh and the media's scrutiny of Serena Williams reveal the unique convergence of racist/sexist stereotypes of Black womanhood. Stereotypes, such as the strongblackwoman and the angryblackwoman, have notable consequences for Black women and girls. It is imperative to not only refute these myths, as studies such as Walley-Jean's (2009) does but to actively work to remove these stereotypes from prevailing discourses about Black girls. It is not enough to recognize a school to prison pipeline exists for Black girls. We must interrogate and eradicate the ways in which stereotypes contribute to disparate treatment of school-age Black girls. By turning to the media and a well-known celebrity, we can see how these stereotypes function in numerous arenas and in conjunction with one another. Media plays a significant role in shaping ideas about race, gender, class, sexuality, ability, etc. The same stereotypes of Black womanhood: impervious to pain and irrationally angry circulate in both mass media and in schools.

The contexts in which stereotypes about Black women and girls thrive are interconnected. To ignore the impact of media on perceptions of Black girls is to miss a ripe opportunity for deconstructing myths and revising policies rooted in harmful stereotypes. The video of #AssaultAtSpringValleyHigh should raise questions about how schools engage Black girls. We cannot afford to look at this assault as an isolated incident, but within a broader context of racist policing, the school to prison pipeline, and a living history of racial/gender stereotypes about Black women and girls. Moving beyond stereotypes of Black womanhood necessitates examining both everyday and spectacular sites of Black girls traversing the world.

REFERENCES

Araton, H. (2015, August 27). Williams sisters leave an impact that's unmatched. *The New York Times.* Retrieved from http://www.nytimes.com
Brown, R. N. (2013). *Hear our truths: The creative potential of Black girlhood.* Urbana, IL: University of Illinois Press.

Chase, C. (2016, July 3). Angry Serena Williams taunts Wimbledon crowd: "Don't try me." *USA Today.* Retrieved from http://www.usatoday.com

Childs, E. C. (2005). Looking behind the stereotypes of the "angry Black woman": An exploration of Black women's responses to interracial relationships. *Gender and Society, 19*(4), 544–561.

Collins, P. H. (1998). *Black feminist thought: Knowledge, consciousness, and the politics of empowerment.* New York, NY: Routledge.

Craven, J. (2015, December 17). The girl who was assaulted by a cop at Spring Valley High on camera is now facing charges. *The Huffington Post.* Retrieved from http://www.huffingtonpost.com

Crenshaw, K. W., Ocen, P., & Nanda, I. (2015). *Black girls matter: Pushed out, overpoliced and underprotected.* Retrieved from http://www.atlanticphilanthropies.org/app/uploads/2015/09/BlackGirlsMatter_Report.pdf

Douglas, D. D. (2012). Venus, Serena, and the inconspicuous consumption of Blackness: A commentary on surveillance, race talk, and new racism(s). *Journal of Black Studies, 43*(2), 127–145.

Faussett, R., Dillman, L., & Glover, S. (2003, September 15). Tennis stars' sister killed in shooting. *Los Angeles Times.* Retrieved from http://articles.latimes.com/2003/sep/15/local/me-williams15

Golding, S. (2015, October 26). Watch as a Spring Valley High School officer violently removes a student from a classroom. *Vibe.* Retrieved from http://www.vibe.com

Harris-Lacewell, M. (2001). African American women's political attitudes and the myth of Black women's strength. *Women and Politics, 23*(3), 1–33.

Harris-Perry, M. V. (2011). *Sister citizen: Shame, stereotypes, and Black women in America.* New Haven, CT: Yale University Press.

King, D. K. (1988). Multiple jeopardy, multiple consciousness: The context of a Black feminist ideology. *Signs, 14*(1), 42–72.

Kirwan Institute. (2016). *Understanding implicit bias.* Retrieved from http://kirwaninstitute.osu.edu/research/understanding-implicit-bias/

Morris, M. (2016). *Pushout: The criminalization of Black girls in schools.* New York, NY: The New Press.

O'Shea, M. (2010, February 9). *The two sides of the Serena Williams coin: The arrogant ace?* Retrieved from http://bleacherreport.com/articles/342391-the-two-sides-of-the-serena-williams-coin-arrogant-but-ace

Roberston, I. (2015, October 28). Details emerge about the Spring Valley High assault victim. *Vibe.* Retrieved from http://www.vibe.com

Romero, R. (2000). The icon of the strong Black woman: The paradox of strength. In L. C. Jackson & B. Greene (Eds.), *Psychotherapy with African American women: Innovations in psychodynamic perspectives and practice* (pp. 225–238). New York, NY: Guilford.

Sargent, A. (2016). *7 lies we have to stop telling about African American girls.* Retrieved from https://mic.com/articles/87985/7-lies-we-have-to-stop-telling-about-african-american-girls#.4KNwdxi1v

Schelzig, E. (2004, March 16). Serena ready to end eight-month layoff. *USA Today.* Retrieved from http://www.usatoday.com

Unsportsmanlike conduct – A portrait of Serena. (2007, October 14). Retrieved from http://www.miamitennisnews.com

Walley-Jean, J. C. (2009). Debunking the myth of the "angry Black woman": An exploration of anger in young African American women. *Black Women, Gender, and Families, 3*(2), 68–86.

Wertheim, J. L. (2004, January 22). Notebook. *Sports Illustrated.* Retrieved from http://www.si.com

Yan, H. (2015, October 29). *South Carolina school officer fired, but more fallout possible.* Retrieved from http://www.cnn.com

Treva B. Lindsey
Ohio State University

GEORGE SIRRAKOS JR.

5. BEYOND A DEFICIT PERSPECTIVE

From the Greek Financial Crisis to Urban Students of Color

INTRODUCTION

Toward the end of the 20th century, poor economic conditions and political turmoil characterized Argentina. In 2008, the United States' real estate market crashed leading to a steep decline in the country's economic activity. Two years later, Greece faced its own financial crisis causing the country to spiral into economic depression. Fast forward to 2016, Great Britain's decision to leave the European Union, colloquially referred to as Brexit, has been greatly scrutinized for its potential impact on global economic markets. Similar to reading the sophisticated literary works of Leo Tolstoy, Herman Melville, and William Shakespeare, understanding the events in Argentina, the United States, Greece, and Great Britain requires their careful unpacking. Unfortunately, I contend that most people may not have the time, desire, or critical acumen to closely examine and discern the root causes and implications of these, and other, global crises, opting instead for limited and superficial understandings of complex happenings.

In similar ways, many school stakeholders (e.g., teachers, counselors, administrators, and school boards) possess narrow and overly simplistic views of the problems that plague urban education and the Black and Brown bodies who typically occupy urban classrooms. In addition, education buzzwords, such as *achievement gap, resilience, college and career readiness*, and *grit,* often distract the general public from engaging in careful and holistic examinations of these problems. As a result, the rhetoric surrounding urban education, and more specifically, urban Black and Brown students, is rooted in misconceptions. For example, some of these misconceptions position Black and Brown students as unwilling to learn and possessing school resistant dispositions that make them unteachable (Emdin, 2016). Other misconceptions situate urban schools as inherently dangerous and violent (Daneshzadeh & Sirrakos, in press). As with all misconceptions, their perpetuation is entrenched in the absence of critical examination.

In this chapter, I use Urie Bronfenbrenner's (1989) ecological systems theory as the framework for understanding contexts through intersecting ecological systems. In particular, I analyze the ongoing financial crisis in Greece to uncover the falsehood that the citizens of Greece are directly to blame for their country's economic condition. As a result, a more nuanced understanding of the situation

G. Sirrakos & C. Emdin (Eds.), Between the World and the Urban Classroom, 53–67.

emerges; one that identifies a variety of external factors, including government corruption and exploitative economic relationships, as culpable. I connect these ideas to the myriad misconceptions and misunderstandings that consistently operate in urban classrooms and shape the academic and social experiences of students of color in those spaces. Thus, I challenge the notion that urban students are directly to blame for their inability to succeed academically and socially in urban classrooms, just as I challenge the notion that the people of Greece are to blame for their country's financial condition. The final section of the chapter interrogates the use of cogenerative dialogues as a pedagogical approach to better understand the ecology of urban classrooms.

THE INTERSECTIONS OF ECOLOGICAL SYSTEMS

As a student of science, I have always been fascinated with the biological concepts of organicism and emergent properties. According to Gilbert and Sarkar (2000), organicism describes the idea that, "properties of any level depend both on the properties of the parts 'beneath' them and the properties of the whole into which they are assembled" (p. 2). Further, emergent properties are described as properties that "cannot be ascribed directly to their component parts but arise only because of the interactions among the parts" (p. 2). For example, the purpose of the heart is to pump blood throughout an organism's body. The heart is composed of cardiac muscle cells organized into cardiac tissue; however, those cells alone do not have the capacity to pump blood. Further, the structure and function of the tissue is dependent upon the organ where it is located. All the while, different organ systems work together to maintain a constant homeostatic balance and prevent the organism's collapse. Given these principles, it is understood that in biological systems, the whole is greater than the sum of each of its individual parts. Similar to biological systems, Bronfenbrenner's (1989) ecological systems theory recognizes the numerous complex interactions and relationships that make up one's identity, referring to these as ecosystems. According to Bronfenbrenner, these tiered ecosystems (i.e., microsystem, mesosystem, exosystem, and macrosystem) influence and are influenced by each other, beginning with an individual's immediate relationships with others and extending to the individual's adoption (or not) of the larger societal values and norms. An ecological examination of one's own identity forces an understanding that moves beyond the most salient points of identity and aims to uncover and explain other, often hidden or unexplored, aspects of the individual's existence. Ecological systems theory provides a framework and approach for a deeper understanding of an individual's contexts in an effort to make sense of how and why an individual feels, thinks, and acts certain ways. In much the same way, I use ecological systems theory to dive deeper into and provide more nuanced understandings of the Greek financial crisis and urban classrooms.

I was very purposeful in selecting the Greek financial crisis as the lens through which I examine perceptions of urban classrooms and students. In reality, the points I make in the remainder of this chapter, likely, could have been made through an exploration of just about any situation or event that is viewed in terms of false binaries and thus oversimplified. I could have opted to discuss the Black Lives Matter movement or the Syrian refugee crisis, but instead I chose to explicate the Greek financial crisis. My reasons for doing so can be best understood through ecological systems theory, namely, that Greece's economic struggles are deeply personal because of my Greek heritage and connection to the country, part of my macrosystem. I am the son of two Greek immigrants who arrived to the United States during the 1960s in search of greater economic opportunities than those available back in their country. Even though my parents had been living in the United States for several years prior to my birth, they made it a priority to instill in me as much of the Greek culture as they possibly could. Thus, ensuring a proper Greek upbringing was, and in many ways continues to be, part and parcel of my microsystem. I was sent to attend a local Greek parochial school where, for at least 3 hours a day, I learned the Greek language and attended classes on Greek mythology, history, and religion. I learned to speak Greek before I could speak English. On Sundays, my family and I attended services at the local Greek Orthodox Church. During snack time, my mother prepared *tiganites*, a delicious peasant snack of fried dough and feta cheese, rather than the traditional American grilled cheese. Religious holidays, such as Christmas and Easter, almost always involved the roasting of a lamb on a spit. By the time I was a teenager, I could speak more intelligently on the 1821 war between Greece and the Ottoman Empire than I could the American Civil War. I think it obvious that, as an adolescent, I strongly identified with being Greek and had a lot of pride in my Greek heritage.

Between 2008 and 2011, I was teaching biology at an international school in Germany. Generally, 2010 is the year most often identified as the beginning of Greece's economic hardships. One morning, as I prepared for my classes, a student came into my classroom and made a snide comment about the deteriorating situation in Greece. He asked, in a voice filled with sarcasm, whether it would be appropriate to hold a school-wide bake sale to help ease Greece's financial troubles. Other students overheard the comment and chimed in by expressing that the economic situation was likely a direct product of the Greeks' overall laziness. One student said, "All Greeks do is drink coffee, smoke cigarettes, and take naps." I was angered by what my students were saying. Whether they made those comments to tease me or because of their sheer ignorance of the situation was irrelevant to me. During that moment, all I understood was that an entire country of people had been unjustly identified as lazy and blamed, whether directly or indirectly, for their country's financial struggles. My response was not what I had wanted it to be, or perhaps it was; until this day, I am still not quite sure. What I mean is that I was torn between two very important aspects of my ecological identity. I valued my position as an educator and, at that point in my life, being a teacher was ingrained as an integral part of my being. Therefore, I knew that my response had to be professional and nonreactive. Simultaneously, my mind flashed back to my family, my ancestors, my heritage, and my experiences. In that regard, all I wanted to do was yell at my students for making such ignorant statements. My teacher identity won this battle, as my response to the students was governed by the ecologically exosystemic and macrosystemic behavioral expectations put in place for newer, expatriate faculty.

AN ECOLOGICAL PERSPECTIVE OF THE GREEK FINANCIAL CRISIS

Greece is a peninsula surrounded by the Aegean Sea to the east, the Ionian Sea to the west, and the Mediterranean Sea to the South. The mainland of southeastern Europe makes up Greece's northern border. Currently, there are approximately 11 million people living in Greece, a country with an area of roughly 52,000 square miles (World Population Review, 2016). For comparison, the United States has a population of approximately 320 million people and an area roughly 74 times that of Greece, with Greece being able to just about fit in the United States' New England region. Greece is also a comparatively smaller country than many other countries in the European Union. Greece is long known for its place in history, its natural beauty, and its prominence as a tourist hotspot, yet anyone who has visited the country in the last decade understands that the country is in economic turmoil. Unfortunately, many have come to believe that the current economic condition in Greece is a result of a nation of people who are unwilling to work for lower wages and consistently mismanage their money. Thus, the people of Greece are often held solely responsible for their country's economic challenges and, as a result, issues such as rising youth unemployment, declining incomes, rising levels of poverty, and drastic cuts to essential services (Rodgers & Stylianou, 2015) are seen as natural microsystemic outcomes of being Greek and living in Greece at this point in time, rather than the result of long-term macrosystemic oppression and exploitation.

In this section, I intend to shift the conversation about Greece's economic crisis by offering a more nuanced understanding, beyond the direct blaming of the Greek people, about what has been happening in Greece over the last several years. To be clear, my purpose is not to offer critical solutions as to what Greece should do to resolve its economic hardships, as I am neither an economist nor a politician. However, let me be blunt when I say that my analysis is rooted in my belief that Greece has been and continues to be plundered. Much like a parasite that feeds off a host organism without killing it, Greece has been on the losing end of a parasitic relationship with the European Union and the Troika, which includes the European Commission, the European Central Bank, and the International Monetary Fund (Troika Watch, 2014). For example, when economic relationships (such as those in the European Union) are driven by neoliberalism and hypercapitalism, then rising inequality, declining wages, and increasing poverty seem to be natural consequences for parasitized countries like Greece (Piven, 2015).

For nearly the past decade, the people of Greece have had to accept the burden of mismanagement by a corrupt and kleptocratic government and the consolidation of their economy by forces external to their nation. When Greece joined the European Union in 2001, its economic demise could have been predicted. Leaving behind a weaker currency for what appeared to be a much stronger one, the Greek government believed that accepting the Euro, and thus aligning with other countries in the European Union, would provide them with economic prosperity. Further, to appease European Union gatekeepers, the Greek government underreported their national deficit, a seemingly common practice among many of the smaller European countries seeking admittance into the European Union (Melvin, 2015).

Over the next few years, the false reporting of Greece's national deficit came in and out of the spotlight and made its entrance to the grand stage in 2007, the year of global economic crises. It was at this point that the discrepancy between money made and money spent hit Greece particularly hard. Greece was in much greater debt than anyone knew or, perhaps more realistically, anyone cared to acknowledge. Rather than allow Greece to default on its monetary loans and place the European Union on an economic collision course, international lenders, led by the Troika, provided Greece with bailout funds (Melvin, 2015). Beyond quelling fears of a European Union collapse, the purpose of the bailout money was to provide Greece with some temporary financial stability in order to allow the country to get its affairs in order. While the funds helped some, Greece's economic problems were far from gone. The economy had shrunk by a quarter in 5 years, and unemployment was about 30% (Polychroniou, 2014). The bailout money received by Greece primarily went toward paying off the country's international loans, mostly interest, rather than making its way into the economy. According to Polychroniou (2013, para. 2), the purpose of such bailouts in a neoliberal European Union is "the pillage of wealth from the periphery to the core of the euro zone." Polychroniou (2014) contends that the Greek bailout agreements will have the following effects:

A catastrophic effect on Greek economy and society while the policies of privatization and structural reforms including radical labor market restructuring have set the stage for the emergence of a type of economy in which economic inefficiency, brutal economic exploitation, severe inequality, foreign dependence and environmental degradation will be the primary characteristics. The claim made here is that the wild neoliberal experiment under way in Greece will produce an economy that will resemble features not of the Celtic Tiger of the mid-1990s to early 2000s—as the current government envisions—but—that of an underdeveloped Latin American country of the 1960s. (para. 4)

The initial bailout agreement was followed by cycles of borrowing money, paying back the interest at astronomical rates, increasing austerity measures, eventually running out of money, and needing another bailout. The impacts of such a vicious cycle were especially felt in 2012, when the amount owed to international lenders comprised 135% of Greece's gross domestic product (Melvin, 2015). The result is a people who have been stripped and demeaned and a country that has become a *financial prisoner* of a neoliberal European Union, or as Viliardos (2016) describes it, "a colony of the lenders" (para. 6). Polychroniou (2013) further describes this phenomenon:

> In our day, bank rescues masquerade as the rescue of nations, followed by the enforcement of unbearable austerity measures for the repayment of the "rescue" loans. Then comes the implementation of strategic economic policies aiming at reducing the standard of living for the working population and the shrinking of the welfare state, complete labor flexibility and the sale of public assets, including state-controlled energy companies and ports. (para. 4)

While Greece has not officially declared bankruptcy, for all intents and purposes, it appears to be and functions as if it is bankrupt. The people of Greece have endured enough in order to assist their country in meeting its financial obligations to lenders. Therefore, it would likely be in the best interest of the people to engage in active forms of resistance and citizenship to envision ways to prevent their country's continued exploitation. Greece is also in a state of political turmoil, yet it is unlikely that any political coup or revolution would actually help Greece's economic situation. The reason for this is that, regardless of the political party elected to lead Greece, the government will continue to be beholden to the Troika, thus perpetuating Greece's economic troubles (Viliardos, 2016).

My analysis of the Greek financial crisis may not be robust enough for some. However, through this counter narrative, I was able to bring to light some underdiscussed, yet complex and important, ecological relationships between the people, their government, and larger financial institutions. In many ways, I wish that I could go back in time and provide my former student with such an understanding. Perhaps it would cause him to trade in his simplified perceptions regarding the people of Greece and instead opt for a more nuanced understanding of the country's economic turmoil.

AN ECOLOGICAL PERSPECTIVE OF URBAN CLASSROOMS AND URBAN STUDENTS

Today's urban schools and classrooms are complex environments that have greatly evolved over the last several decades. However, to the general population, the word "urban" evokes specific images and feelings. Wright and Alenuma (2007, as cited in Kareemo & Conti, 2012) explain that,

> "Urban" has become a euphemism for schools with exclusively or predominantly poor student of color populations (especially Black and Latino) and connote schools that are characterized by underfunding, racial and economic segregation, inefficient administration, poor infrastructure, demoralized teaching faculty, poor equipment, resources, and facilities, overcrowded classrooms, outmoded and largely ineffective pedagogical approaches, student on student and student on teacher violence, chronic classroom management problems, dilapidated and/ or dangerous neighborhoods, uninvolved and uncaring parents, etc. (p. 212)

Rather than thinking about and describing urban schools through a strengths-based perspective, the current discourse in the United States conceives of urban schools as spaces that are bursting with troubles and deficits as illustrated by Wright and Alenuma. Thinking about urban schools and classrooms in such a narrow manner perpetuates the notion that urban classrooms are culturally, socially, and academically deficient, particularly when compared to their suburban school counterparts, thus further marginalizing urban classrooms and the students of color who most often occupy them. Unfortunately, viewing people of color, including children in urban classrooms, through a deficit lens is as American as apple pie. In the United States, this way of thinking stems from a legacy of colonialism, where White settlers enslaved Africans, used them for their labor, pillaged Native American tribes, and stole sacred land (Feagin, 2002). The repercussions of colonialism are thought to be long gone. After all, the United States government has agreed to numerous land treaties with various Native American tribes, the landmark *Brown v. the Board of Education of Topeka, Kansas* (1954) desegregated American public schools, the Black suffrage movement became a reality in 1965 when the Voting Rights Act was signed into law, the No Child Left Behind legislation aimed to help low-achieving schools become academically successful, and in 2008, the people of the United States elected the country's first Black president, Barack Obama. White people, being on the apex of the social hierarchy, view these acts as proof that the United States' history of colonialism is extinct. In doing so, they tend to dismiss the pervasiveness of colonialism and White supremacy as current and active hegemonic structures (hooks, 1994) that result in culturally subtractive school experiences (Valenzuela, 1999), particularly for our country's most marginalized youth. Lea and Edouard-Gundowry (2014) explain that,

Hegemony is the process through which we learn to see the social narratives that support the interests of those in power—oligarchies and plutocracies—as normal, natural, and commonsense, even when they do not equate with our interests. Colonialism, racism, and Whiteness are hegemonic processes. In fact, hegemony leads us to vilify poor and immigrant people—disproportionately people of color—and support policies that maintain their economic oppression. We even blame some poor and immigrant parents, who are challenged in terms of economic and language resources and may not share the cultural assumptions of the mainstream, for not helping their children to prepare for and function in school. In other words, we have little sense of the ways in which society was set up by people already socially and culturally advantaged to maintain their own advantage. (p. 185)

Hegemony in urban classrooms manifests in myriad ways, many of which go unquestioned and, therefore, undisturbed. Some examples of this include the lack of focus on exploring critical Whiteness in urban teacher preparation programs (Matias & Zembylas, 2014); funding disparities between urban and suburban schools (Ostrander, 2015); approaches to discipline that perceive urban students of color as being in need of restoration (Daneshzadeh & Sirrakos, in press); the promotion of standardized curricula that are neither challenging nor engaging (Milner, 2012); and pedagogical approaches that lack cultural responsiveness and, instead, rely on compliance to strict rules that subjugate urban students of color (Emdin, 2016). Because these issues often remain unexplored, urban students of color continue to be directly blamed for their perceived inability to succeed academically and for possessing antischool dispositions, even though schooling in America was never meant to serve students of color (Oakes, Stuart Wells, Jones, & Datnow, 1997). Thus, academic and behavioral success for urban students of color are often judged "in terms of certain Anglocentric, cultural, symbolic, linguistic, and economic standards, including northern European norms of beauty; traditional, direct, individualistic, verbal, and nonverbal communication styles" (Lea & Edouard-Gundowry, 2014, p. 186).

The works of Gloria Ladson-Billings, H. Richard Milner, and Tara Yosso, among many others, help to further explicate ecological perspectives of urban students and the classrooms they occupy. In particular, their works offer educators, researchers, and theorists alternative frameworks to the all-too-well-known *achievement gap* between White students and students of color. In her 2006 American Education Research Association presidential address, Ladson-Billings implored the education community to explore and understand achievement, particularly for students of color, in schools in the United States in terms of an *education debt*, a conception that attempts to make sense of why an achievement gap exists to begin with. Ladson-Billings argues, "the historical, economic, sociopolitical, and moral decisions and policies that characterize our society have created an education debt" (p. 5). By understanding the "legacy of educational inequities in the United States" through these four debt types that have long victimized communities of color, then "an achievement gap is a logical outcome" (Ladson-Billings, 2006, p. 5). Building on the notion of an education debt, Milner (2012) asserts that gaps in achievement can be further understood through an exploration of opportunity gaps. Milner asks, "Why do so many educational researchers focus on outcomes rather than on the processes that lead to the outcomes?" and goes on to explain that, "Issues related to opportunity are complicatedly multifaceted, process oriented, and much more nuanced than what an achievement gap explanation can provide" (p. 696). Thus, Milner lays out five core, interrelated microsystemic, exosystemic, and macrosystemic tenets of the opportunity gap framework. These are (a) the influence of color blindness, (b) cultural conflicts in the classroom, (c) the myth of meritocracy, (d) low expectations and deficit mindsets for students of color, and (e) context-neutral perspectives that fail to recognize the social contexts of schools and communities. Jacqueline Jordan Irvine (2010, as cited in Milner, 2012) identifies specific structural and systemic opportunity gaps, particularly for students of color, in terms of the following:

> The teacher quality gap; the teacher training gap; the challenging curriculum gap; the school funding gap; the digital divide gap; the wealth and income gap; the employment opportunity gap; the affordable housing gap; the health care

gap; the nutrition gap; the school integration gap; and the quality childcare gap. (p. xii)

In *Whose Culture Has Capital? A Critical Race Theory Discussion of Community Cultural Wealth,* Tara Yosso (2005) suggests that the White normative narrative permeating urban public schools is in opposition to the ways of knowing and being for Black and Brown students. If urban classrooms are to become spaces where students of color can seek and attain academic success, then the hegemonic classroom structures that oppress them need to be challenged. According to Yosso, this must begin with an acknowledgement and focus on the "array of cultural knowledge, skills, abilities and contacts possessed by socially marginalized groups that often go unrecognized and unacknowledged" (p. 69). Yosso challenges the belief that students of color come from culturally deficient communities meaning that they themselves must be culturally deficient. Instead, Yosso asserts that students of color and the communities from where they come "nurture cultural wealth through at least 6 forms of capital such as aspirational, navigational, social, linguistic, familial, and resistant capital" as a means to "survive and resist macro and micro-forms of oppression" (p. 77).

For many urban educators, understanding the education debt, uncovering opportunity gaps, and leveraging forms of community cultural wealth are perpetual and complex challenges. In the remaining sections, I draw parallels between the Greek financial crisis and urban classrooms and offer cogenerative dialogues as an approach to realize Ladson-Billings's, Milner's, and Yosso's visions. As has been the theme of this chapter, it is my hope that students will be viewed by their strengths and capabilities, while educators acknowledge how the proverbial "deck of cards" is stacked against students of color in the forms of an education debt and opportunity gaps.

CONNECTING THE PIECES

The Greek financial crisis and the current state of oppression of Black and Brown youth in urban classrooms would likely not be two phenomena that most people would draw parallels between. While I focus on a single connection, readers will likely draw additional connections beyond the one I make. In this section, I focus on the persistence of deficit perspectives as a result of lack of accountability of oppressive macrosystemic structures as manifested in Greece's current economic situation and urban classrooms.

When I began researching the events leading up to Greece's economic collapse, I could not help but be bothered by the Troika's role in dismantling the Greek economy. In many ways, the Troika functions in much the same way as neoliberal hypercapitalist ideology does in the United States and beyond. Acting as a monetary lender, the Troika, perhaps more covertly than overtly, positioned itself as the savior of Greece. The money provided by the Troika gave the people of Greece a false sense of stability and freedom. People were given just enough access to resources to believe that their lives remained unchanged and that the ability to make choices regarding their lives continued to rest with them. However, the truth is that the Troika has imprisoned the people of Greece and placed upon them *financial shackles* that not only prevent them from improving but also cause the deterioration of the quality of their own lives. This is particularly true for Greece's working class who have been subjected to harsh austerity measures, decreased wages, cuts in pensions, and long-term unemployment. However, to the rest of the world, these citizens continue to be viewed from a deficit perspective; a group of people who simply do not want to or lack the ability and motivation to do better for themselves. Thus, I assert that the Troika is synonymous with the construct of neoliberal hypercapitalism in that it functions to keep the dominant class intact while simultaneously having little regard for the country's most vulnerable class of citizens.

The United States government, in many respects, functions in much the same way. Legislation and policy consistently demonstrate that the success of Black and Brown students, particularly those attending urban schools, is not a priority. Similar to the Troika, neoliberal hypercapitalism persists under the guise of superficial reform efforts, such as No Child Left Behind, to perpetuate thinking of students of color in terms of deficits. As is, neoliberal hypercapitalist ideology would not dare disrupt the status quo by tackling the macrosystemic problems that plague urban schools. Thus, rather than investing in the infrastructure of urban communities, investing in high-quality teachers, investing in increasing employment opportunities, investing in increasing social and rehabilitation services rather than for-profit prisons, and investing in communities who work to dismantle the school-to-prison pipeline, the United States government would rather invest in bailing out big banks in order to allow hegemonic classism to persist in American culture.

COGENERATIVE DIALOGUES AS DISRUPTORS OF URBAN CLASSROOM HEGEMONY

Ideally, the classroom environment should function as a space where information can be exchanged fluidly. However, this is often not the case, particularly in urban classrooms populated primarily by students of color (Noguera, 2008). Instead, exchanges of information are dominated by the teacher with little, and often superficial, reciprocation from the students (Emdin, 2009). As Yosso (2005) described, the knowledge and perspectives that an urban teacher possesses are often held in higher regard and perceived to be the norm. Conversely, the cultural capital and others ways of knowing and being for students of color are often disregarded and not perceived as having any value in the educational space. This discrepancy leads to the perpetuation of classroom hegemony, particularly in the form of deficit-thinking. Ladson-Billings (1994) writes:

> Most teacher candidates do not need an immersion experience in white middle-class culture because they are either products of it or have been acculturated and/or assimilated enough to negotiate it successfully. However,

when beginning teachers come into minority communities, many are unable to understand the students' home language, social interaction patterns, histories, and cultures. Thus, they cannot truly educate the students. Their perceptions of deficiency and competence are socially and culturally constructed. Without greater exposure to the students' culture, teachers lack the tools with which to make sense of much that transpires in the classroom. (p. 134)

Cogenerative dialogues have been used in classrooms for nearly 2 decades to bridge the cultural disconnects that are often present between teacher and students (Roth, Lawless, & Tobin, 2000). Cogenerative dialogues reveal to teachers how their pedagogical practices, language, and implicit biases work together to maintain oppressive classroom learning environments. As a result, cogenerative dialogues function to jointly produce and reproduce a counter-hegemonic classroom culture that acknowledges the impact of oppression and actively challenges and disrupts classroom systems of oppression, including those related to race, gender, class, ethnicity, and language. During cogenerative dialogues, there is an "emphasis and importance placed upon participants' shared responsibility to prioritize the classroom conditions that promote learning" where "each constituent informs the other, without having to presuppose the other" (Bayne & Scantlebury, 2013, p. 239).

As the term *cogenerative dialogue* implies, these are out-of-class conversations where participants, in most cases a small group of students and their teacher, jointly generate plans of action that explore "teaching in particular ways, rationale for events and practices, and commitments to practices that emerge and conform to particular values and ethics" (Tobin, 2006, p. 138). Further, the group of students who participate in the cogenerative dialogues should be heterogenous in some way. For example, one student may be a high-achieving student, one student may be a lower-achieving student, another may be an English language learner, and another may be a student athlete (Emdin, 2016). This is to ensure the presence of diverse perspectives that can actively challenge hegemonic structures present in the urban classroom.

According to Emdin (2016), successful cogenerative dialogues need to be governed by established protocols. First, the physical space should be arranged in a manner that allows all participants to see each other and ensures all participants feel comfortable and included in the conversation. Second, there must be an expectation of equal turns at talk with no voice being privileged over another. This is particularly important for the teacher who is likely accustomed to holding a privileged voice in the classroom. Next, the participants must agree to a plan of action that everyone, teacher and students, are responsible for enacting. Finally, there must be an expectation that cogenerative dialogues are an ongoing, reflective, and iterative process. By engaging in consistent and ongoing cogenerative dialogues, the teacher demonstrates her authentic commitment to learning about her students and teaching in ways that are reflective of students' funds of knowledge (González, Moll, & Amanti, 2005). Simultaneously, the students demonstrate to their teacher that they possess specific insider knowledge and significant expertise in the distinct domain of the classroom. As a result, deficit perspectives of students begin to be challenged and erased.

In a study by LaVan and Beers (2005), a student participant in cogenerative dialogues pointed out that the conversations benefited the classroom and the individual student in that it gave him,

> A chance to hang out with and get to know teachers and students in a very real way. We get to build social capital and have fun at the same time. We are not sitting there being fake, but talking about interesting things that relate to all of us. (p. 162)

LaVan and Beers (2005) concluded that cogenerative dialogues "generally encourage students to use multiple and varying resources (human, symbolic, and material) while observing, describing, and communicating understandings of the circumstances to others, supporting ideas with evidence, and listening to others' perspectives" (p. 162).

My own research (Sirrakos & Fraser, 2016) along with the findings from a plethora of other teachers and researchers (Bayne & Scantlebury, 2013; Emdin, 2007, 2011, 2016; LaVan & Beers, 2005; Seiler, 2001; Seiler & Elmesky, 2007; Tobin, 2006; Tobin, Elmesky, & Seiler, 2005; Tobin & Roth 2005) have uncovered several positive outcomes of cogenerative dialogues. These outcomes include ways in which the teaching and learning process have changed for both the teacher and students. I identify some of these outcomes below:

- Acknowledgement of student social capital
- Production of student-emergent curricula
- Creation of a cosmopolitan classroom ethos
- Decrease in classroom behavior issues
- Expansion of the role of students in the classroom to function as co-teachers
- Fostering of collaborative, peer-to-peer relationships
- Inclusion of pedagogical practices that are responsive to the needs of students
- Opportunities for students to express their emotions and creativity
- Increased knowledge of place and local history
- Teaching and practicing teamwork and distributed leadership
- Creation of citizens who see the value in helping others succeed
- Pooling of expertise to enhance teaching and learning
- Providing authentic learning experiences and assessments

The common thread among these outcomes is that they demonstrate the strengths of urban students of color. These strengths become evident when students of color are included in the teaching and learning process, rather than excluding students and perpetuating the fallacy that they are intellectually deficient and unable to achieve academic success.

Cogenerative dialogues hold much promise, however, the practice is often met with apprehension and mistrust on the part of students. Teachers may misconstrue these reactions as a lack of maturity or unwillingness to engage in the process on the part of students. However, Emdin (2016) asserts that, to some degree, students are likely validated in harboring feelings of mistrust toward such conversations. For what has likely been most of students' academic careers, teachers have been making decisions about students without any input from the students. In the rare instances in which students try to insert their voices, they are often perceived as trying to avoid doing work. As a result, teachers feel the need to "settle students and regain control" (LaVan & Beers, 2005, p. 149). Therefore, successful participation in cogenerative dialogues requires a teacher who is ready to engage in genuine "reflection on where they stand in reference to what students think of the classroom" (Emdin, 2007, p. 322).

CONCLUSION

The purpose of this chapter was to urge urban educators to pursue broader ecological understandings of their students. Beginning with an analysis of the financial crisis in Greece, I demonstrated the need for individuals, both part of and external to the situation, to wrestle with and engage with more meaningful understandings that push beyond the microsystem and instead begin to make sense of the exosystem and macrosystem. In turn, I used this framework to bring to light that urban Black and Brown students are often viewed in terms of deficits. That is, they possess ways of knowing and being that are not valued by, and seemingly incompatible with, the larger, dominant societal (coded as White, Anglosaxon, heteronormative) ways of knowing and being. Borrowing from Paul Gorski's (2013) idea of *equity literacy*, urban educators need to move beyond deficit perspectives of students and instead cultivate,

> The ability to recognize both subtle and not-so-subtle biases and inequities in classroom dynamics, school cultures and policies, and the broader society, and how these biases and inequities affect students and their families; the ability to respond to biases and inequities in the immediate term, as they crop up in classrooms and schools; the ability to redress biases and inequities in the longer term, so that they do not continue to crop up in classrooms and schools; and the ability to create and sustain a bias-free and equitable learning environment for all students. (p. 21)

I offer cogenerative dialogues as a mechanism for the inclusion of multiple voices in the work toward equity literacy. Through cogenerative dialogues, students and their teacher work together to find suitable solutions, in the form of plans of action, for classroom problems. The nature of these solutions is such that they work to move beyond and dismantle hegemonic classroom structures. They provide teachers with the tools to uncover their students' strengths while providing students with opportunities to demonstrate their academic potential. Further, the cogenerative dialogues make known to students the broader ecological systems that function to keep urban communities of color oppressed. Thus, students recognize these systems within their classrooms and schools, and also within their communities, instilling within them a desire to, as my students might say, "*get woke.*"

REFERENCES

Bayne, G., & Scantlebury, K. (2013). Using cogenerative dialogues to expand and extend students' learning. In B. J. Irby, G. Brown, R. Lara-Alecio, & S. Jackson (Eds.), *The handbook of educational theories* (pp. 239–250). Charlotte, NC: Information Age Publishing.

Bronfenbrenner, U. (1989). Ecological systems theory. In R. Vasta (Ed.), *Annals of child development* (Vol. 6, pp. 187–249). Boston, MA: JAI Press.

Brown v. the Board of Education of Topeka, Kansas, 347 U.S. 483 (1954).

Daneshzadeh, A., & Sirrakos, G. (in press). Restorative justice as a double-edged sword: Conflating restoration of Black youth with transformation of schools. *Taboo: The Journal of Culture and Education.*

Emdin, C. (2007). Exploring the contexts of urban science classrooms: Part 1–Investigating corporate and communal practice. *Journal for Cultural Studies of Science Education, 2*, 319–341.

Emdin, C. (2009). Rethinking student participation: A model from hip-hop and urban science education. *Edge Phi Delta Kappa International, 5*(1), 1–18.

Emdin, C. (2011). Moving beyond the boat without a paddle: Reality pedagogy, Black youth, and urban science education. *The Journal of Negro Education, 80*, 284–295.

Emdin, C. (2016). *For White folks who teach in the hood ... and the rest of y'all too: Reality pedagogy and urban education.* Boston, MA: Beacon Press.

Feagin, J. R. (2002). White supremacy and Mexican-Americans: Rethinking the "Black-White paradigm." *Rutgers Law Review, 54*, 959–987.

Gilbert, S. F., & Sarkar, S. (2000). Embracing complexity: Organicism for the 21st century. *Developmental Dynamics, 219*, 1–9.

González, N., Moll, L., & Amanti, C. (2005). *Funds of knowledge: Theorizing practices in households, communities and classrooms.* New York, NY: Routledge.

Gorski, P. C. (2013). *Reaching and teaching students in poverty: Strategies for erasing the opportunity gap.* New York, NY: Teachers College Press.

hooks, b. (1994). *Teaching to transgress: Education as the practice of freedom.* New York, NY: Routledge.

Kareemo, T., & Conti, J. (2012). Working within and around urban school bureaucracy. In A. J. Stairs, K. A. Donnell, & A. Hadley Dunn (Eds.), *Urban teaching in America: Theory, research, and practice in K-12 classrooms* (pp. 181–206). Thousand Oaks, CA: Sage.

Ladson-Billings, G. (1994). *The Dreamkeepers: Successful teaching for African-American students.* San Francisco, CA: Jossey Bass.

Ladson-Billings, G. (2006). From the achievement gap to the education debt: Understanding achievement in U.S. schools. *Educational Researcher, 35*, 3–12.

LaVan, S. K., & Beers, J. (2005). The role of cogenerative dialogue in learning to teach and transforming learning environments. In K. Tobin, R. Elmesky, & G. Seiler (Eds.), *Improving urban science education: New roles for teachers, students, and researchers* (pp. 147–164) Lanham, MD: Rowman & Littlefield.

Lea, V., & Edouard-Gundowry, M. S. (2014). Targeted by the crosshairs: Student voices on colonialism, racism, and Whiteness as barriers to educational equity. In A. Ibrahim & S. S. Steinberg (Eds.), *Critical youth studies reader* (pp. 184–194). New York, NY: Lang.

Matias, C. E., & Zembylas, M. (2014). "When saying you care is not really caring": Emotions of disgust, Whiteness ideology, and teacher education. *Critical Studies in Education, 55*, 319–337.

Melvin, D. (2015, July 13). Between rock, hard place, Greece picks austerity. How did it get into this mess? *Cable News Network*. Retrieved from http://www.cnn.com/2015/07/13/europe/how-greece-reached-this-point/

Milner, H. R., IV. (2012). Beyond a test score: Explaining opportunity gaps in educational practice. *Journal of Black Studies, 43*, 693–718.

Noguera, P. (2008). *The trouble with Black boys: And other reflections on race, equity, and the future of public education.* New York, NY: Wiley.

Oakes, J., Stuart Wells, A., Jones, M., & Datnow, A. (1997). Detracking: The social construction of ability, cultural politics, and resistance to reform. *Teachers College Record, 98*, 482–510.

Ostrander, R. R. (2015). School funding: Inequality in district funding and the disparate impact on urban migrant school children. *Brigham Young University Education and Law Journal, 2015*, 271–295.

Piven, F. F. (2015). Neoliberalism and the welfare state. *Journal of International and Comparative Social Policy, 31*, 2–9.

Polychroniou, C. J. (2013, March 27). Imperial Germany and the pillage of Europe's indebted Mediterranean region. *Truthout*. Retrieved from http://www.truth-out.org/opinion/item/15348-imperial-germany-and-the-pillage-of-europes-indebted-mediterranean-region

Polychroniou, C. J. (2014, January 19). The Greek "success story" of a crushing economy and a failed state. *Truthout*. Retrieved from http://www.truth-out.org/news/item/21265-the greek-success-story-of-a-crushing-economy-and-a-failed-state

Rodgers, L., & Stylianou, N. (2015, July 16). How bad are things for the people of Greece? *British Broadcasting Corporation*. Retrieved from http://www.bbc.com/news/world-europe-33507802

Roth, W.-M., Lawless, D. V., & Tobin, K. (2000). {Coteaching/cogenerative dialoguing} as praxis of dialectic method. *Forum Qualitative Sozialforschung/Forum: Qualitative Social Research, 1*, Article 37.

Seiler, G. (2001). Reversing the "standard" direction: Science emerging from the lives of African American students. *Journal of Research in Science Teaching, 38*, 1000–1014.

Seiler, G., & Elmesky, R. (2007). The role of communal practices in the generation of capital and emotional energy among African American students in science classrooms. *Teachers College Record, 109*, 391–419.

Sirrakos, G., & Fraser, B. J. (2016). A mixed-method, cross-national study of reality pedagogy. *Learning Environments Research: An International Journal.* doi:10.1007/s10984-016--y

Tobin, K. (2006). Learning to teach through coteaching and cogenerative dialogue. *Teaching Education, 17*, 133–142.

Tobin, K., & Roth, W.-M. (2005). Implementing coteaching and cogenerative dialoguing in urban science education. *School Science and Mathematics, 105*, 313–322.

Tobin, K., Elmesky, R., & Seiler, G. (2005). *Improving urban science education: New roles for teachers, students, & researchers.* Lanham, MD: Rowman and Littlefield.

Troika Watch. (2014, February 11). Troika under scrutiny: European parliament joins CSOs. *Troika Watch*. Retrieved from http://www.troikawatch.net/troika-under-scrutiny-european-parliament-joins-csos/

Valenzuela, A. (1999). *Subtractive schooling: U.S.-Mexican youth and the politics of caring.* New York, NY: State University of New York Press.

Viliardos, V. (2016, August 14). [Occupation]. *Analyst.gr*. Retrieved from http://www.analyst.gr/2016/08/14/katohi/

World Population Review. (2016). *Greece population 2016.* Retrieved from http://worldpopulationreview.com/countries/greece-population/

Yosso, T. J. (2005). Whose culture has capital? A critical race theory discussion of community cultural wealth. *Race, Ethnicity, and Education, 8*(1), 69–91.

George Sirrakos Jr.
Kutztown University of Pennsylvania

6. DESTROYING THE SPECTACLE IN URBAN EDUCATION

Embracing the New Danger

In 2004, rapper Mos Def released an album entitled *The New Danger*, which stunned many album critics who were expecting the hard-hitting beats and rhymes that were synonymous with traditional rap albums and Mos Def's previous work. On the album, he experimented with funk, rock, and soul music and covered subject matter that ranged from the commercialization of Hip Hop by corporations to loss and heartbreak. The body of work Mos Def produced moved beyond what typical commercial rap audiences and record companies expected. In response, he was critiqued harshly by album reviewers and the general public for not following the existing and expected script. Consequently, the sonically brilliant and rich in Black musical tradition album was regarded as "an awkward ill advised stumble" (Warren, 2004, para. 1). Mos Def's decision to explore other genres of music that went beyond the expected focus of rap/Hip Hop even though they were invented by Black artists and part of his musical lineage was hard to accept by tastemakers in music. One album reviewer described it as "more of a collage than a collective statement" that "immediately places it in unfavorable context" (Henderson, 2004, para. 1).

Reviewers failed to recognize that Mos Def's exploration of funk, rock, and soul was his attempt to connect back to Black origins of music in a climate in which record companies were only selling and promoting a very distinct form of rap music that featured similar beats, a narrow subject matter in the rhymes, and prefabricated stories about urban America and the ghetto lifestyle that came with it. Mos Def engaged in a battle for a more complex identity by creating a form of musical expression that pushed against the prescribed formula for a successful rap album by expanding what a rap album could be inspired by and speak about. He could have certainly followed the existing script and guaranteed himself the attention and adulation from the music industry. If he chose to do so, he would grace magazine covers and be celebrated. However, this attention would have been predicated on his acceptance that his full identity as historian, rock artist, blues singer, and poet had to be sacrificed. His visibility in an industry that had defined what a successful rap artist looked and sounded like required fitting into an identity constructed by the world around him. Record labels needed their rappers to be Black, violent, angry, and ignorant drug dealers (Perry, 2004). They could sell and profit from that

G. Sirrakos & C. Emdin (Eds.), Between the World and the Urban Classroom, 69–81.

narrative easily. Anything other than that would not work because it would shatter preconceptions held by society writ large about what it means to be a Black male in urban America. For that population, their societally constructed identity does not include being students of genres of music beyond rap. It does not call for deep social analysis and critiques of the system like Mos Def's revelation that "old White men is running this rap shit; corporate forces is running this rap shit" (Mos Def, 2004, track 5). Rather, it is predicated on (and perpetuates) an ignorant populace who relegate themselves to socioeconomically challenged communities and engage superficially in politics and education (Kelley, 1996).

This phenomenon of making a negative or flawed narrative about a group of people hypervisible while rendering their full selves invisible and profiting from the flawed narrative has permeated every corner of Americana. It is present in global narratives about criminal immigrants taking advantage of citizens when those immigrants are taken advantage of as sources of cheap labor (Luibheid, 1997; Rosello, 2001), women being perceived as less effective than men in the workplace despite their being overqualified so that women can be given lower wages than their male counterparts (Elson & Pearson, 1981; Tannen, 1994), and urban youth of color being presented as disinterested and perpetually underperforming in school (Emdin, 2007) that I argue has a goal of allowing testing companies and school start-up companies to profit from the underperformance they identify. These false narratives have become much more visible in the current political era and over the course of the election of Donald Trump as President of the United States. Over the course of Donald Trump's campaign, he made Black and Brown people visible for the sake of implanting or affirming false flawed narratives about them to the public. As these communities are discussed on the largest and most public political stages, the state of African American communities and the presence of Latino/a immigrants are tied directly to the threat that these communities pose to the safety and livelihoods of White America. In other words, rather than discussing or describing the complexities of these communities, or their contributions to society, they are framed as a perpetual problem and danger to White segments of the population who are made to be fearful of an America where they are no longer the majority. Blackness and Brownness then become visible only when a single and flawed narrative of what they are gets described to the world, and counter narratives that are more complex and layered are harshly critiqued and dismissed as inauthentic.

This is the same process that Mos Def underwent when he created his album *The New Danger* and is indicative of what Debord (1967) describes as the spectacle. Debord goes on to explain that under the spectacle, "everything that has been directly lived has receded into a representation" (p. 1). In other words, the lived experience of a particular group is never directly seen or understood, but other people's views of it become reality. In its current iteration, the spectacle has become an anchor of the strategy of the political elite. It has become the tool through which reality becomes disfigured so that a false reality can become attractive. It sells negative images of a complex culture to a public who has grown so accustomed to receiving false truths that authentic narratives that counter the spectacle seem false. Consider, for example, "the successful Haitian Revolution [that] was ignored by history because it imposed a totally different narrative, which rendered the dominant slave narrative of the day untenable" (Peck & Baldwin, 2017, p. 1). Also consider the shifting of narratives in the recent exchange between Donald Trump and Congressman John Lewis.

Congressman John Lewis is a civil rights icon who rode interstate buses into segregated states as part of the Freedom Riders movement during the most hostile social and political environment of the United States (Bausum, 2008). Congressman Lewis was beaten and arrested numerous times in his fight for civil rights and was present for a number of the most iconic civil rights marches in the history of the United States. Since then, he has remained a champion for many causes for the disadvantaged as a congressman who represents a district in Atlanta that covers a diverse socioeconomic, ethnic, and racial demographic. Congressman Lewis, in an interview about Donald Trump, shared his sentiments about the illegitimacy of Trump as president (Todd, Bronston, & Rivera, 2017). This sentiment was publicly shared by many on both sides of the political aisle in response to the spectacle Trump created around Black and Latino/a communities, urban neighborhoods, and immigration. In response to Congressman Lewis, Trump doubled down on the spectacle approach to influencing the public by attempting to delegitimize the congressman and constructing a narrative about him and those he represents that attempted to devalue the congressman's accomplishments. This narrative was also designed to construct an image of a poor and crime-ridden congressional district run by someone who is, as Trump described Congressman Lewis in a tweet, "all talk, talk, talk—no action or results" (Trump, 2017). Trump's description of Congressman Lewis, who had protested, been assaulted, and fought tirelessly for social justice, as a man of "no action or results" served as one of the most visible and offensive efforts by a world leader to reconstruct a narrative about a citizen in recent history. However, in some sick and twisted way, Trump's recrafting of Congressman Lewis's past serves as unquestionable evidence of the nature of the spectacle within contemporary America and the ways that it targets and distorts the complex narratives of people of color. More specifically, if a man whose history of action and service is well known and highly respected can be dismissed and turned into a talking head by the person who sits at the head of the nation, any anonymous person of color without a public presence and visible history can easily be turned into much worse.

For folks of color in this country, their life endangering actions toward being fully seen have always been relegated to "talk, talk, talk" by those who hold power. At the same time, narratives about the conditions that spurred on the actions (now dismissed as empty talk) are either skewed or erased completely. A meaningless term like postracial has been forced down the throat of people who are crying for a recognition of their humanity. The structural and institutional racism they experience daily is somehow hidden under popular phrases about progress and greatness. The mere mention of the reality that we do not exist in a postracial society gets presented as radical. Those who argue for their complex narratives and truths to be seen get positioned as agitators. The spectacle then is "where the real world changes into simple images," and "the simple images become real beings" (Debord, 1967, p. 18). Under the spectacle, complex histories get distorted, realities get caricatured, and the caricatures that get created become real in the eyes of a public who is more comfortable with images than real people. In a society that operates under the spectacle, a freedom fighter from the civil rights era like Congressman Lewis gets transformed into a useless relic from a distant and insignificant past.

The example of the spectacle that opened this chapter described how Mos Def was robbed of an opportunity to be more that just a rapper by a music industry that saw him in a simplistic way that did not allow for a full expression of his humanity. In much the same way, the spectacle has functioned in politics to sell the idea to the public that there are people who do not deserve to be seen as full citizens. No exemplary personal or collective action can exempt them from being positioned as being in opposition to those who have the right to have their full humanity expressed. Whether we are discussing rappers, members of Congress, or everyday citizens, the spectacle functions to not only strip a person or group of their depth and complexity but makes a commodity of the positions they currently hold in the imaginations of the public to profit the orchestrator of the narrative. In the case of Mos Def, record companies profited from him being a rapper from an urban neighborhood who did nothing more than rap. He was critiqued for pushing beyond the identity that was constructed for him because the new more complex self he expressed on *The New Danger* could not be sold back to the public writ large in the form of albums. The more complex identity Mos Def offered on *The New Danger* and the new narratives that that identity surrounded itself with challenged the public perception that he, and others like him, were "just rappers."

In much the same way, Trump profited from constructing an "immigrant problem" that casts millions of hard-working people as inherently dangerous. By painting wide swaths of the population as dangerous, he benefited politically by selling these images to a public who feeds into the hysteria that is generated by the creation of a false threat to their livelihood. What was most fascinating about the spectacle in recent politics is the use of demonization of one group to be framed as care for another more powerful group. For example, the identification of Mexicans as rapists and drug dealers (Trump, 2015) was sold as caring for the American people. Immigration laws that see no value in Latino/a immigrants are sold as a means to protect American jobs for "everyone." As exemplified in a number of Trump's speeches from his election campaign to the presidency, mistruths were spread because the spectacle allows for lies to become truths as long as they are told in a way that plays to the public's fear of the "other" as implanted in the public's psyche through the consistent retelling of false narratives. Alternative facts get constructed simply by the retelling of falsehoods, and truths that should emerge from critically analyzing data and making meaning of the full human experience get misinterpreted and dismissed as falsehoods. Debord (1967) describes this process as détournement—the "reradicalization of previous critical conclusions that have been petrified into respectable truths and thus transformed into lies" (p. 206). For example, a Trump phrase used repetitively over the course of the election was that "the African Americans [or other ethnic or racial group] love me," which runs counter to evidence that ranges from polling data to mass protests that indicate the exact opposite. To counter the truth that reality presents, a single African American man in a sea of hundreds was called out by Trump as "my African American" even though he was not a Trump supporter, and a pair of African American women were given visibility as they played out neck swinging and finger snapping caricatures of Blackness while endorsing Trump.

In many ways, the existing approach to urban education follows this same model when engaging the public on schools and schooling. Flawed narratives about the academic/intellectual challenges of urban youth of color, the underperformance of all their schools, and the dysfunction and violence in their communities are presented concurrently with inauthentic yet highly publicized narratives about wanting to improve the circumstances/conditions of these young people. It is through this sleight of hand where a narrative of wanting to make the conditions better for populations often described as downtrodden is used to ensure that a segment of the population is perpetually seen as downtrodden that power maintains itself through the spectacle in politics and in urban education.

LIVING THE URBAN EDUCATION SPECTACLE: A SCHOOL VISIT

After receiving a brochure that boasted of a new school's diverse teaching staff and innovative approaches to instruction, I walked into a middle school in a newly renovated building in a newly gentrified urban neighborhood to witness gleaming hallways and a flat screen greeting visitors who walked into the building. The images on the screen were of students of color who wore bright smiles and freshly pressed uniforms with hands raised and an air of confidence on their faces. After signing the guest book and walking down an empty well-decorated hallway, the sounds of an intense exchange between a young boy and his teacher bounced off the halls, and I was drawn to their interaction. I was startled not by the fact that the teacher and student were in a loud exchange, but by the nature of the interaction between the White male teacher and the Latino boy who looked up at his teacher and asked for answers to questions that seemed to be so much larger than the ones the teacher was offering him. "I don't care what is going on outside of class. You're going to be on your best behavior in here," the teacher said. As I peeped into classrooms on my way to the main office, and with the exchange I observed between the teacher and student still on my mind, I noticed the racial demographics in the school. The students were mostly African American and Latino/a, and the teachers were mostly White. The few teachers of color seemed to blend into the backdrop, and the students and their racial identities were made very visible. The Black and Brown faces of the students were there in the flesh, on the flyers, and on the flat screen televisions that decorated the walls. However, despite how visible the students were, their community and culture were absent. The school administration and staff had found ways to erase the neighborhood and the community while highlighting the fact that the students were youth of color from "tough neighborhoods." The socioeconomic challenges that the students faced were highlighted, but the beauty and resolve that were also a part of the community were nowhere to be found.

In this school, like many others across urban America, there is a belief that good schools do not look or feel like their surrounding community. For youth to be successful in school and in life, they are expected to leave their real lives at the door and mold themselves into versions of their teacher or their school that are far from who the students truly are. This appears to make sense to the public and teachers who believe in the narrow and negative descriptions of youth and their lives and in their own abilities to transform these lives for "the better." However, hidden in their beliefs about changing the lives of youth is the lack of value they have for youth and their communities. These educators, in many ways, believe themselves and their institutions to be better than the youth and their communities. There is a certain hubris that is at the core of much of urban education that has grown to become integral to how institutions operate.

In my book, *For White Folks Who Teach in the Hood ... and the Rest of Y'all Too* (Emdin, 2016), I highlight the ways that White teachers are recruited for teaching in urban schools through teacher recruitment initiatives that utilize narratives about how downtrodden and unfortunate the students are as the chief means to get the socioeconomically advantaged in society to "give back" to the less fortunate by teaching. This process is a replica of the spectacle in politics and music and has implications for how these teachers engage with youth, their parents, and their communities. Teachers who walk into classrooms with a belief that their students are broken and in need of heroes to save them from their dire circumstances do not see their students as whole and capable people. For these people, narratives that see the worst in students but hold teachers as kind and caring givers guide teaching. Teaching then becomes part of the same spectacle that allows politicians to demonize entire segments of the public because these populations are seen as worthless. When groups of people are perceived as worthless, it is easy for them to be experimented on. Models where one can recruit and place underprepared college graduates and career changers without any serious preparation for teaching or any true knowledge of the lives of urban youth into urban classrooms to teach become widely accepted practices (Ladson-Billings, 1999). What many fail to recognize is that these legitimized models are rooted in the belief that communities of color lack value and that schools within those communities are to teach students to fit into dominant culture or be like the teacher (who has no true appreciation for urban youth and their traditions). This process, often enacted by people from racial and ethnic backgrounds that do not reflect those of their students, are most insidiously implemented by educators of color who have been put in place by schools to maintain the flawed narratives about youth of color (Emdin, 2016). Just as Trump (2016) identified and highlighted "my African American" in the midst of a rally filled with

White faces despite the fact that the Black person who was there didn't know or support him and just as he endorsed Black people who caricatured Blackness and did not represent the larger sentiment of the community, a new shift toward improving urban education that places Black and Brown faces in visible roles within a system that is intent on demonizing full cultural expressions of Blackness and Brownness has taken root. The spectacle once again becomes evident even as it uses well-intentioned White liberal, Black middle class, and Brown upwardly mobile bodies to maintain its function to demonize urban America.

THE NEW SCHOOL BULLIES

In urban communities across the country, efforts to recruit educators have taken on a dangerous form that involves a pleading to the "kind-hearted nature" of the affluent. In many cases, aspiring lawyers and doctors with little to no connection to urban communities are seduced into the teaching profession by institutions that pitch narratives about how bad, poor, broken, and in need of help urban youth are. College graduates are told that a short term "giving back" to "the most unfortunate" will provide them with loan forgiveness while benefitting them in their future life plans and professional goals beyond the classroom. This self-serving and ego-driven charity donor mentality is the major recruitment narrative for many urban schools and sets the stage for thousands of teachers to go into classrooms believing that they are heroes for placing their initial career goals on hiatus for youth of color. These new teachers walk into classrooms not only holding on to the perception that urban youth of color are inherently damaged, disadvantaged, and in need of restoration, but these inexperienced teachers believe that they are the ones to save their students from themselves and their poor neighborhoods. This savior narrative is embedded in the flawed notion that the best education in urban spaces requires replicating the structures of the teachers' own education. Replicating norms from the teachers' own experiences or their communities does not improve the lives of urban youth whose realities often have no connection to those of their teachers. Teachers whose knowledge of urban youth of color comes from media constructed narratives that are an aggregate of those constructed by the spectacle in media and politics (as described in the examples with Mos Def and Donald Trump) are doomed to exercise the bias that is at the root of the spectacle. A teacher who has only seen rap video renditions of Blackness approaches Black youth with an expectation of a very particular way of expressing self and almost expects that type of expression in order to be comfortable. If students come to the classroom enacting behaviors that run counter to those constructed by the spectacle, they are erased in favor of those that reinforce the teacher's expectations. In this system, the false narratives of the spectacle get projected onto students, and they begin learning that they are only accepted when their behaviors reinforce negative stereotypes. For example, a teacher who sees students as violent even though the students do not condone violence may ultimately incite students to react violently. This, in many ways, is the danger of the spectacle. It moves people out of their realities and toward behaviors that have been constructed about them. Once these people enact any behavior that reinforces any semblance of the negative stereotype, the behavior is then used to justify and reinforce the negative stereotype.

Just as the spectacle plays out in urban classrooms in the relationship between teacher and student, it also plays out in the current era where public schools are publicly demonized by proponents of charter schools that are headed up by well-intentioned philanthropists hell-bent on giving better options to the downtrodden youth in traditional urban schools who need saviors from their current plight. These narratives are exemplified in the infamous movie *Waiting for Superman*, which played on the sympathy of the public and the narratives about how bad urban communities are to garner attention for "better" schools. This simple yet powerful narrative erases any alternatives beyond saving the poor kids because it serves to reinforce the perception that they need saving and that those who save them are superheroes. The decision to privatize schools erases options like supporting communities in creating their own schools, investing in the improvement of existing schools, and reimagining curriculum and assessments so that they reflect the culture and community of the young people. The issue with exploring these options is that it would place power and control in the hands of the community and that would require a belief that they were valuable enough to be invested in or to control their own narratives. As people like Trump's first Education Secretary, Betsy DeVos (who have no direct interactions with urban communities or urban public schools but are being charged with the highest national seat in education) use wealth and a narrative of care for the downtrodden to push for removing community control from schools, the spectacle that uses "good intentions" to demonize urban communities plays out openly in contemporary urban education.

The system of education must acknowledge that improving urban education requires that we must first lift the dangerous veil constructed by the spectacle. This begins with training teachers to understand the dangers of blindly accepting curriculum, standards, school rules, and mission statements that may have ulterior intentions from what they are presented to have. It also requires informing communities about the ways that their desires for a better education for their children are being used to satisfy narratives of caring for the unfortunate that many private entities use to argue about how good they are and what great charity they provide. What the spectacle has been able to do in education is construct narratives that exaggerate the ineffectiveness and/or danger of traditional urban public schools by extending the flawed narratives of urban communities to the schools within them. Concurrently, the spectacle glorifies narratives about the effectiveness of alternatives to urban public schools that erase the ineffective pedagogies enacted within them. When record companies reduce Blackness to rap and when politicians reduce it to destitution, educators cannot follow suit and reduce urban education to savior narratives aimed at maintaining deficit views of urban youth.

NEXT STEPS: ON OTHERING AND BECOMING

The path toward uprooting the spectacle begins with a general populace who is critical of messages that are being sent by institutions that hold power and is self-reflective about how they may be complicit in affirming or maintaining false narratives. It is in many ways what Greene (1978) describes in her essay "Wide-Awakeness and the Moral Life" as "living with one's eyes open" (p. 43) or existing in a state of wide-awakeness. I argue that having one's eyes open means that we question narratives that we are being locked into and question how and why we are complicit in the spectacle by asking questions about phenomena that we take for granted. An example of the questions we must pose to invoke wide-awakeness and subvert the spectacle was captured by Hall (1980) in a deconstruction of a magazine cover that was framed innocently but was delivering a very particular and preferred alternate message. Asking ourselves what the preferred meanings are opens up the space for the following questions that Hall (2001) suggests we ask in order to move beyond the spectacle:

- How do we represent people and places that are significantly different from us?
- Why is difference so compelling a theme, so contested an area of representation?
- What is the secret fascination of otherness and why is popular representation so frequently drawn to it?
- What are the typical forms and representational practices used to represent difference in popular culture today, and where did these popular figures and stereotypes come from?

When these questions are applied to urban education, many underexplored truths about the nature of teaching and learning and the larger movement to privatize urban public education become apparent. For example, any interrogation of how urban youth of color are represented in media, research, or documents related to education reveals images and text that tie these youth to criminal behavior, violence, and disinterest in education. Even research articles that focus on urban youth are often front-loaded with data that highlight their academic underperformance and frame them as being significantly different from "normal" students who are not explicitly named as but are generally understood to be White and upper middle class.

If educators are engaging in work that allows them to trouble how they view students, their engagements with them shift significantly. Furthermore, the idea of difference and why it is such an important piece of why and how we teach inevitably emerges. When educators in urban spaces confront difference in schools and begin to ask why difference is anchored on youth of color being seen as less than and other, they begin to see their roles in maintaining the narratives constructed by the spectacle. Otherness in urban education is the secret component of the problematic teacher recruitment narrative and the seemingly perpetual academic underperformance of youth of color. The perception of urban youth of color as other than the norm (with the norm often reflecting the teacher's perception of self) is what allows narratives about these students' deficiencies to take root. Teachers who see themselves as the norm also see themselves as good, kind, and smart. When students do not share the same experiences or backgrounds as their teacher, the teacher sees the students as the other. When students get positioned as the other, they are seen as the opposite of how teachers see themselves and become, in the teachers' mind, bad, mean spirited, and unintelligent. Teachers' flawed perceptions of students are birthed from any number of differences (e.g., cultural, racial, socioeconomic, or otherwise) that exist because students are positioned as the other. These perceptions get reinforced and affirmed by narratives that are constructed and shared by and through the spectacle, which trigger the negative perceptions of urban youth that we have all become too comfortable with.

The work for educators who have become aware of the spectacle and the myriad of ways that it limits the potential of urban youth to be more than the world imagines them to be is to work with their students to uproot and expose it. Most importantly, this requires a deliberate effort to enact pedagogical practices that are aimed at creating contexts that empower youth to speak back against the ways that the spectacle is being experienced by them in the classroom. I suggest that these types of classroom spaces may serve as triggers for empowering youth to address larger issues beyond the classroom. For example, a young man of color who is only seen as an athlete because of his size and race who begins to see himself as academically gifted in a democratic classroom operates in the world differently with this newfound knowledge about his ability. In much the same way, a young woman in an urban classroom who is only affirmed for being quiet and docile who gets an opportunity to have her voice heard in a democratic classroom, operates differently in the world beyond it. This process requires approaches to teaching and learning that provide educators with tangible tools for detaching themselves from their allegiances to institutions and creating democratic classrooms where students feel like full citizens, such as reality pedagogy (Emdin, 2011). Full citizenship in urban education imagines the classroom as its own world where there is a social condition where young people have the agency to escape whatever limitations are placed on them in the larger society. Through a reimagining of the classroom and the role of urban youth within it, students are given the license to push back against how they are being treated in the classroom with a goal of pushing back against how they are viewed in the world beyond the classroom. I argue that the freedom to critique the world at large and position oneself as central in how you are perceived is a "new danger" to the status quo. Just as Mos Def's album *The New Danger* pushed back against what record labels expected or desired from him, classrooms and schools can and should do the same. The tools for reality pedagogy include cogenerative dialogues, coteaching, cosmopolitanism, context study as an anchor for instruction, content being delivered in ways that connect to content, competition that builds community and camaraderie among students, and curating and studying artifacts from the classroom (Emdin, 2016). Of these seven steps, the first three are specifically designed to serve as tools for both the awakening and empowerment of young people around the spectacle and its impact on their lives.

Cogenerative dialogues are conversations with young people in groups of four to six about both their classroom and the world at large with a goal of improving a shared experience (Emdin, 2007; Tobin & Roth, 2005). While these dialogues usually revolve around academic content and may be disconnected from sociopolitical issues beyond the classroom, the teacher may trigger an exchange around larger issues beyond the classroom by asking general questions often removed from classroom discussions related to how they believe they are perceived in the media, their opinions about race and politics, and their thoughts on how they are being perceived and taught in the school/classroom. The goal here is for the educator to ask these questions and then step back to allow the youth to not only share their thoughts/ concerns but also consider whether the ways they have been described/positioned in the world aligns to the ways they see themselves. Critical conversation then becomes regular classroom practice that when enacted consistently, naturally reveals the existence of the spectacle and its effects on urban youth of color to youth of color. Once youth become aware of the spectacle and their role within it, it becomes essential that they have an outlet for sharing the information they have newly discovered and constructively releasing the emotions that naturally emerge. This is why I suggest that the critical cogenerative dialogue be married to coteaching, which provides opportunities for youth to use what Rumala, Hidary, Ewool, Emdin, and Scovell (2011) describe as a community-based participatory approach that positions youth as experts on their community and their own experiences and culture. Once students have deconstructed the ways they have been perceived by society through their discussions of race, class, and education, they become awakened to the nature of the spectacle. Once the realization of their positions in society become apparent, they must be given the opportunity to teach. Coteaching in reality pedagogy allows youth to be teachers. They take the helm of the classroom, design lessons on the topics they want to share, and the opportunity to teach allows for the co-exploration of themes that emerge from their critical cogenerative dialogues with the rest of the class. Once students take on this role, and their teachers get repositioned as peers, there is a shift in the ways that youth see themselves, and they begin to construct identities that go beyond the ones that exist for them within the spectacle. Finally, and perhaps most importantly, it is essential that cosmopolitan classroom spaces are created—where youth can forge deep connections to each other and the classroom and use this space to launch an assault on the spectacle by redefining what it means to be urban. Cosmopolitan learning spaces are framed less like traditional urban classrooms and take on more of the structure of families. There is less focus on sitting quietly, being docile, passively learning, and working individually. Instead, there is a focus on asking questions, being actively engaged in what is being discussed, and forging relationships with and connections to the people who are part of the family.

Once these three steps happen in succession first, and then in tandem, a perfect storm of sorts is created that becomes a threat to the spectacle. Once critical cogenerative dialogues that challenge students to question how they are being viewed/ treated are in place and when students begin to teach and see themselves as teachers, they gain support from peers in cosmopolitan classrooms who encourage each other to challenge the status quo. When criticality and wide-awakeness is triggered and youth begin to see themselves as more than what they have been constructed to be, they become a new danger to the spectacle and those who benefit from it. To be seen as a danger to systems that hold power and maintain it for themselves by painting negative and inauthentic images of wide swaths of our population is, in many ways, the true goal of education.

REFERENCES

Bausum, A. (2008). *Freedom riders: John Lewis and Jim Zwerg on the front lines of the civil rights movement*. Prince Frederick, MD: Recorded Books.

Debord, G. (1967). *Society of the spectacle*. Detroit, MI: Black and Red.

Def, M., (2004). *The new danger* [CD]. New York, NY: Geffen Records.

Elson, D., & Pearson, R. (1981). 'Nimble fingers make cheap workers': An analysis of women's employment in third world export manufacturing. *Feminist Review, 7*, 87–107.

Emdin, C. (2007). *Exploring the contexts of urban science classrooms: Cogenerative dialogues, coteaching, and cosmopolitanism* (Unpublished doctoral dissertation). City University of New York, New York, NY.

Emdin, C. (2011). Citizenship and social justice in urban science education. *International Journal of Qualitative Studies in Education, 24*, 285–301.

Emdin, C. (2016). *For White folks who teach in the hood ... and the rest of y'all too: Reality pedagogy and urban education*. Boston, MA: Beacon Press.

Greene, M. (1978). Wide-awakeness and the moral life. In M. Greene (Ed.), *Landscapes of learning* (pp. 42–52). New York, NY: Teachers College Press.

Hall, S. (1980). Encoding/decoding. In S. Hall, D. Hobson, A. Lowe, & P. Willis (Eds.), *Culture, media, language: Working papers in cultural studies, 1972–79* (pp. 128–138). London, England: Hutchinson.

Hall, S. (2001). The spectacle of the 'other.' In M. Wetherell, S. Taylor, & S. Yates (Eds.), *Discourse theory and practice: A reader* (pp. 324–344). London, England: Sage.

Henderson, E. (2004, October 19). Review of Mos Def's The New Danger. *Slant Magazine.* Retrieved from http://www.slantmagazine.com/music/review/mos-def-the-new-danger

Kelley, R. (1996). *Race rebels: Culture, politics, and the Black working class*. New York, NY: Simon and Schuster.

Ladson-Billings, G. (1999). Preparing teachers for diverse student populations: A critical race theory perspective. *Review of Research in Education, 24*, 211–247.

Luibheid, E. (1997). The 1965 Immigration and Nationality Act: An "end" to exclusion? *Positions, 5*, 501–522.

Peck, R., & Baldwin, J. (2017). *I am not your Negro*. New York, NY: Vintage Books.

Perry, I. (2004). *Prophets of the hood: Politics and poetics in hip-hop*. Durham, NC: Duke University Press.

Rosello, M. (2001). *Postcolonial hospitality: The immigrant as guest*. Redwood City, CA: Stanford University Press.

Rumala, B. B., Hidary, J., Ewool, L., Emdin, C., & Scovell, T. (2011). Tailoring science outreach through e-matching using a community-based participatory approach. *PLOS Biology, 9*, e1001026. Retrieved from http://dx.doi.org/10.1371/journal.pbio.1001026

Tannen, D. (1994). *Talking from 9 to 5: How women's and men's conversational styles affect who gets heard, who gets credit, and what gets done at work*. New York, NY: William Morrow and Company.

Tobin, K., & Roth, W.-M. (2005). Implementing coteaching and cogenerative dialoguing in urban science education. *School Science and Mathematics, 105*, 313–322.

Todd, C., Bronston, S., & Rivera, M. (2017, January 14). Rep. John Lewis: 'I don't see Trump as a legitimate president'. *NBC News Meet the Press*. Retrieved from http://www.nbcnews.com/meet-the-press/john-lewis-trump-won-t-be-legitimate-president-n706676

Trump, D. J. (2015, June 16). Presidential announcement speech. *Time*. Retrieved from http://time.com/3923128/donald-trump-announcement-speech/

Trump, D. J. (2016, June 3). Campaign speech. *CNN*. Retrieved from http://www.cnn.com/videos/politics/2016/06/03/donald-trump-rally-african-american-kkk-sot.cnn

Trump, D. J. (2017, January 14). [Twitter moment]. Retrieved from https://twitter.com/realDonaldTrump/status/820255947956383744

Warren, J. (2004, October 18). Review of Mos Def's The New Danger. *Pitchfork Magazine*. Retrieved from http://pitchfork.com/reviews/albums/5441-the-new-danger/

Christopher Emdin
Teachers College, Columbia University

7. BEYOND BEATS, RHYMES, & BEYONCÉ

Hip Hop, Hip Hop Education, and Culturally Relevant Pedagogy

For more than 25 years I have been studying the pedagogical practices of teachers who are successful with African American students. My rationale for this inquiry came from my early days in graduate school where it seemed everything I read discussed the near impossibility of teaching poor, Black children. I read studies that suggested that poor, Black families were dysfunctional and incapable of raising healthy, happy children able to achieve in school classrooms. I read other studies that suggested that poor, Black communities were so chaotic that it was impossible for them to produce productive citizens who would contribute positively to the economic and political body politic of the society.

Some of the more "enlightened" studies I read argued that no matter what we did, schools were unable to overcome the huge "cultural deficits" that existed in poor, Black communities. Indeed, the notions of "cultural deficit" and "cultural deprivation" took hold in the scholarly community and became the explanation for Black school failure. The "remedy" became cultural "compensation" and by the mid-1960s we witnessed the birth of a range of compensatory education programs such as Head Start and Follow Through. The rationale that undergirds these programs was if school personnel could "get a hold" of poor, Black children earlier (i.e., get them away from their mothers, families, and communities), they might have a chance to undo all of the negative influences of the students' home and community lives. We began seeing a rash of studies that argued Black mothers did not talk to their babies enough and when they did, they did not say the "right" things. Other studies pointed to a lack of toys in the home of poor Black babies and toddlers, and that lack apparently signaled limited opportunities for intellectual stimulation. A counter study by Hale-Benson (1986) argued that when Black researchers went into the homes of Black families they observed plenty of toys, but those toys were typically in a playpen or toy box while the babies were being constantly held by the adults and other older children in the household. Their conclusion was that this interaction helped Black children to be more people-oriented rather than object-oriented.

Finally, by the 1980s some scholars began talking about a notion of "cultural difference" (rather than cultural deficits) to suggest that there were some fundamental differences between students' home cultures and that of the schools. However, identifying cultural differences rarely produced curricular or instructional strategies

G. Sirrakos & C. Emdin (Eds.), Between the World and the Urban Classroom, 83–94.

that could improve achievement. Instead, a new set of stereotypes often emerged suggesting the students were so "different" that it was difficult for "mainstream" teachers to reach them. All of these characterizations of poor, Black children irritated me in a very particular way, primarily because I grew up in an urban community as a "poor, Black child." Yet, I was succeeding in graduate school in one of the nation's most prestigious institutions of higher education, AND I could attribute much of my success to the nurture of my community, a number of elementary teachers, and a spectacular education in a Historically Black College/University. It was difficult for me to accept that I was so unusual, so special, so unique that this could only happen to me. I was convinced that there were teachers who understood how to reach and teach poor, Black students without destroying their basic humanity—their sense of Blackness.

ORIGINS OF CULTURALLY RELEVANT PEDAGOGY

It was fortuitous that I chose to minor in anthropology in graduate school. There I learned about the complexity and intricacies of the concept "culture." By studying a variety of traditional and more isolated cultures, I learned that culture was not merely the tangible artifacts (e.g., art, literature, languages, tools, music, religious practices, and technologies) that groups created but also the cosmologies; modes of thinking; world views and orientations toward knowledge, truth, and evidence. I began to understand that the culture I grew up in and learned was not limited to only what could be seen. It was also embedded in me. I, like everyone else, was a "culture-carrier." However, none of us have access to the full range of our culture(s), and we often are selective in when, where, and how we access it. For instance, when I began attending an integrated junior high school, I became less willing to use my home language and mannerisms because it seemed to cause my middle-class, White classmates to exclude and sometimes ridicule me. In the process, I became what scholars call, "bicultural." I had a home language and a school language or what Gee (2014) calls a primary discourse and a secondary discourse. And, I quickly learned that school valued the secondary discourse that Delpit (2006) calls "the culture of power."

I credited my academic success to the teachers who supported my home culture while simultaneously exposing me to the mainstream culture. What did these teachers know and how did they do this? This was what I wanted to know. Could we document the pedagogical expertise of teachers who were successful with developing this bicultural perspective? More specifically, could I find those teachers capable of developing what King (2005) called a "relevant Black personality?" I did not realize it at the time, but I was asking a fundamentally different kind of question. Instead of constantly asking what was wrong with poor, Black children, I wanted to know what was "right" with poor, Black children and what happens in classrooms where teachers help them succeed on a regular basis (Ladson-Billings, 2009).

Over a period of 3 years, I spent countless classroom hours observing a group of eight outstanding teachers (both Black and White) who had a track record of proven success with Black (as well as Latinx[1]) students. Although their pedagogical practices—techniques, strategies, etc.—varied, I soon learned that their philosophies and belief systems were quite similar. It was here that I learned that much of the fuss over "methods" was misplaced. What teachers believe about their students, their families, and communities matter immensely. Instead of feeling sorry for their "poor," "disadvantaged," "at-risk" students, the teachers in my study focused on the strengths and assets students brought to the learning environment. The ability to see students' strengths came from a deep connection to the students' culture and the school community. The Black teachers seemed to recognize the strength and resilience in the students because they had seen it in their own experiences growing up. The White teachers had taken the time to get to know the families and community and realized that many of the parents were doing much more with their meager resources than their own families had done with much more. In addition to getting to know the students, families, and community, the teachers in my study also had a strong understanding of themselves as teachers. They had strong self-efficacy and expected to be successful with their students. Later, Martin Haberman (2005) would call teachers like them "star teachers."

My work to distill the practice of these excellent teachers became what is known as "Culturally Relevant Pedagogy." The three propositions of this theoretical construct are academic achievement or more precisely student learning, cultural competence, and sociopolitical consciousness or critical consciousness. Academic achievement or student learning refers to the knowledge, skills, and intellectual dispositions that students acquire as a result of their schooling experiences. I want to be clear that student learning is much more than student performance on standardized tests that many equate as achievement. Student learning includes a clear delineation of what students can do when they enter a classroom and what they can do at any point beyond that (i.e., end of a month, semester, or year).

Cultural competence addresses the ability for students to be well grounded in their home culture(s) and fluent in at least one additional culture. Grounding in the home culture includes knowledge of the history, traditions, values, and language of the home culture(s). For many urban students fluency in another culture typically refers to being able to access the dominant culture, but it does not mean relinquishing or denigrating one's home culture. Developing facility in both cultures helps to create a bicultural student who is comfortable in multiple contexts.

Sociopolitical consciousness or critical consciousness refers to the ability of students to offer thoughtful critique about what they are learning in school and what they are experiencing in society. A culturally relevant teacher is likely to draw from out-of-school issues to help students develop their critical consciousness. For example, in the midst of the civil unrest in communities like Ferguson, Missouri and Baltimore, Maryland, culturally relevant teachers asked what students were thinking and feeling about these events. A culturally relevant teacher would then offer students information from a variety of perspectives so that they could come up with more informed analyses of what transpired. Such teachers may also help students decide what kind of civic and social action they want to engage in. This work would make use of the literacy, numeracy, historical, and scientific information they have learned in the classroom. These three components—student learning, cultural competence, and critical consciousness—are the absolute basic elements of culturally relevant pedagogy. Without these elements, people are not practicing what I have come to know and understand as culturally relevant pedagogy.

CULTURALLY RELEVANT PEDAGOGY REMIXED

Now, some 25 years past my early explorations into this phenomenon of culturally relevant pedagogy, I am challenged to re-examine the concept and consider what seem to be some obvious shortcomings. People must remember that I focused my inquiry in elementary classrooms. I did that because the self-contained classroom was less complex and I could see the development of long-term relationships between teachers, students, and families. I could see teachers working with students in various subject areas. I could see 5–6 hours a day of work with the same group of students. But, I could not see fully the influence of youth culture on these young students. At the secondary level, I would have seen students' incorporation and reinterpretation of popular culture in their daily lives and whether their teachers chose to capitalize on this particular cultural knowledge. Younger students have some access to youth culture but typically consume it rather than shape it the way adolescents do. Consequently, when I saw teachers making use of home culture (which they did regularly), they pulled on cultural history, family traditions, and community customs. For example, the community where I conducted my study participated in Juneteenth celebrations. Juneteenth is a commemoration of the June 19, 1865 arrival of Union soldiers in Galveston, TX to alert enslaved African Americans that slavery was over. This was two and a half years past the January 1, 1863 signing of the Emancipation Proclamation. Today, Juneteenth is celebrated in Black communities across the nation.

But, few of the teachers in my study used the power of youth and popular culture to inform their teaching. Today, secondary teachers are working with young people who are the embodiment of youth culture. Their deep engagement in youth culture informs how they see and experience the world. This engagement has to be a part of any reconceptualization of culturally relevant pedagogy. But I must confess a fear of any wholesale appropriation of youth culture—especially Hip Hop—into the typical school classroom. This is not because I have fears about the significance or content of Hip Hop but rather a fear of distortion and misappropriation of the art by those who do not truly understand it and see it as a gimmick or "hook" to "motivate" "poor," "urban," and "at-risk" students. My fear is rooted in a concern for the integrity of the art. I worry that teachers eager to maintain order in a classroom will attempt to *use* Hip Hop as a pacifier rather than a learning tool and strategy. I consider the work of Nasir (2011) who investigated Black males' use of mathematics while playing basketball and dominoes. Nasir pointed out that although the young people were deeply involved in these out-of-school activities, the worst thing teachers could do would be to take the students' leisure activities and turn them into school activities. Thus, a teacher who would use Hip Hop in the classroom must first become a student of Hip Hop.

BECOMING HIP HOP

Instead of trying to become a Hip Hop head, I am hoping to see teachers become Hip Hop in their orientation to pedagogy. My own "conversion" came as a result of talking to a number of students of color—mainly Black and Latinx—who were a part of my university's award winning, First Wave Hip Hop Arts Scholars Program. Many of these students were from urban communities in Atlanta, Chicago, Detroit, Milwaukee, New York, Oakland, and other cities. A significant number of the students expressed a desire to teach and integrate their artistry in their teaching. Unfortunately, nothing in our existing teacher education program made space for that kind of expression. Student after student expressed frustration at sitting in classrooms with mostly White, middle-class, suburban students who thought of "urban education" and teaching in city schools as dangerous and undesirable. Additionally, the faculty members contributed to the stereotypical and distorted notions of who "urban" students are. Frustrated and angry, the students began dropping out of the teacher education program and deciding on post-baccalaureate alternative programs that provided limited preparation.

After meeting with the students and our First Wave director, we decided that we could at least offer a course or two that helped students understand how they could integrate their art and education. The result of our meetings was the development of two course offerings. The first course was "Pedagogy, Performance and Culture" and the second course was "Pedagogical Flows: Hip Hop in the K-12 Classroom." In each course I reserved half of the seats for members of First Wave and half for the general student population. Both courses were also paired with our "Getting Real" speakers series where we brought in amazing intellectuals and artists to speak to the class and deliver public lectures. Among our speakers were Coleman Domingo (of film, TV, and stage), Michael Cirelli (Director of Urban Word), Dawn-Elissa Fisher and Dave "Davey D" Cook (San Francisco State), Ebro Darden (on-air DJ and former NYC Hot 97 Program Director), Christopher Emdin (Teachers College, Columbia University), Mark Anthony Neal (Duke University), Elaine "Docta E" Richardson (Ohio State University), Martha Diaz (New York University), H. Samy Alim (Stanford University), Brittany Cooper (Rutgers University), and Marc Lamont Hill (Morehouse College).

In order to teach this course, I had to study up. I was already an "adult" when Hip Hop emerged in popular culture. I grew up as a "soul," "rhythm and blues," and "jazz" aficionado. I studied music and grew up in a household where music was omnipresent. I was a part of the "Motown" generation and of course, as a Philadelphian—"The Sound of Philadelphia." I went to school with Dee Dee Sharp, who would become the first wife of Kenny Gamble (of Gamble & Huff). The original "American Bandstand" program aired from my neighborhood at 46th and Market Streets before it migrated to the West Coast. When the Sugar Hill Gang released "Rapper's Delight" I was a teacher with children of my own. My experience with "spoken word" came from the militant voices of the 1960s, especially "The Last Poets": Amiri Baraka, Haki Madhubuti (then known as Don L. Lee), Sonia Sanchez, and June Jordan. To me, Hip Hop was a part of what we would now call, "house music," not to be sold or consumed commercially, but a vehicle for relief from the hostility and tension that built up in our community. Hip Hop was something you went to the streets or dance parties to hear, not something to be bought in a record store.

Part of my preparation was reading Jeff Chang's (2006), *Can't Stop Won't Stop*. The history teacher in me liked that I could put my hands on a reliable and long range view of the art form. Chang starts in Jamaica and links Hip Hop to its Rastafarian roots. Here I came to understand the political underpinnings of the movement. It was a way to restore the spoken word, always sacred in the Black community. Our heroes have always been wordsmiths—Frederick Douglas; Sojourner Truth; Martin Luther King, Jr.; Fannie Lou Hamer; Malcolm X (el Hajj Malik el-Shabazz); Stokely Carmichael; Audre Lorde; Toni Morrison; and Barak Obama, to name a few. This thing called Hip Hop was just the latest iteration of what had been present in our communities for centuries. One of its innovations was in the crafting of powerful beats to accompany the rhymes. But it also brought an assertive and provocative critique of society and the structural inequality oppressed people faced at every turn.

Following Chang's text, I explored Jay-Z's (2011) *Decoded* along with Tupac Shakur's (2009) *The Rose That Grew From Concrete*, and Forman and Neal's (2011) Hip Hop studies reader *That's the Joint!* In addition to the texts that celebrated Hip Hop, I knew it was important to read work that offered critique. I read Charnas' (2011) *The Big Payback: The History of the Business of Hip Hop* to look at the money trail that emerged when Hip Hop moved from an accessible street art form where artists performed, pressed their own CDs, and sold them from the back of their cars to a multimillion dollar enterprise. I knew enough about the history of the entertainment business to know that many extremely successful Black artists ended up penniless and destitute. Capitalism would do to Hip Hop what it did to all original art forms—rip it off, repackage it, and resell it to the community that had created it in the first place.

Also, I thought it was important to read the ideological and political critiques that developed around Hip Hop. I turned to Tricia Rose's (2008) *The Hip Hop Wars: What We Talk About When We Talk About Hip Hop—and Why it Matters*. Here Rose lays out the basic public arguments, pro and con, about Hip Hop and challenges them. A few of those pro and con arguments include focusing on violence, demeaning women, keeping it real, and failing to discuss positive Hip Hop.

The point of my course was not to have students sitting around listening to their favorite Hip Hop songs but rather to engage Hip Hop as a way to think about how popular art forms shaped our students' thinking and world views. Hip Hop would be both a vehicle and a pedagogical strategy. For me, it would be a way to help culturally relevant pedagogy evolve for 21st century teachers and students. I learned a tremendous amount by becoming Hip Hop that has less to do with a specific music, art, dance, or fashion than it does with what it means to place students' needs first. In the next section of this chapter, I speak to the pedagogical moves becoming Hip Hop helped me to make.

PEDAGOGICAL FLOWS

I have always loved what I call the "pedagogical dance." When it is flowing (or working), there is an amazing back and forth that develops between teacher and students. Sometimes it comes as a result of careful study and planning. Other times it is serendipitous—someone notices or says something, the media covers a news story, or I read something just before entering the classroom. There is no better feeling than when the classroom is flowing. There are times when I have to be deliberate and directive. There are other times when I just have to light the spark and student spontaneity and creativity takes over and spreads throughout the classroom.

Many years ago, when I was a public school teacher I noticed the absence of music in classrooms. For as long as I can remember, I awoke each morning to music. When my older brother was in the Air Force, he sent me one of the first-generation transistor radios with earphones. With the help of a steady supply of batteries, I could listen to music everywhere. I was the coolest girl in my West Philadelphia neighborhood. Later, as a young teacher I drove to my South Philadelphia school with the radio in my Volkswagen Beetle blasting. But, once I crossed the threshold of the school building there was an eerie silence. I decided to take a radio to class and turned it on in the early morning as I prepared for my students. I promptly turned it off when the morning bell rang because that was the school protocol. However, one morning as I finished grading a stack of papers I didn't hear the bell, and I forgot to turn off the radio. Students started streaming in. Quickly, I rose to turn off the radio and one of my students said, "Naw … leave it on, PLEASE!" I left the radio on for a few minutes as students filed in, and I noticed how they grooved to the latest sounds. Some sang along, others bobbed their heads, and no one bothered anyone else. There was not one altercation. No one was picking on another student. No outside-of-the-classroom beefs were apparent. Everyone was just enjoying the music. From that moment on, I began playing music as students entered the class and during selected moments during class.

About a week after the radio experience, I checked out a phonograph (or record player) from the school library and began bringing in albums from home. I included popular rhythm and blues, jazz, blues, and European classical music. I realized that not only was the music soothing but playing it was an opportunity to introduce the students to a wider range of music. I still remember the excitement the students had when we listened to the cast album of the Broadway show, *Hair*. My evidence of the impact of the pedagogical move to include music in the classroom came one day when one of my struggling students made a musical request. Here was this African American boy for whom school had been a horrible experience who responded when I asked the class, "What kind of music do you want to hear while you work on your essays?" "Can you play that—'don-don-don-DON song?—That's my joint!" He was referring to Beethoven's Fifth Symphony. I stood there with my mouth agape and played his selection. In a matter of moments, an entire group of my Black boys were moving their heads to this European classical symphony. The simple act of playing music in the classroom created a pedagogical flow. Department stores, supermarkets, and even elevators understand that human beings crave music in their environments. Schools, on the other hand, work hard to eliminate music from the atmosphere. Imagine places like cafeterias, auditoriums, and other school gathering spaces with music in the background as students enter and exit. In our quest for control, adults have purged the school of one of the simplest forms of creating order—a little music.

From those early years, I never again taught a public school class without the presence of music. Somehow when I moved to higher education, I once again left music out of the classroom. But, when I began teaching the "Hip Hop course," I realized once again how important it was to create a playlist. Although many of my students were avowed Hip Hop heads, few knew the early music and my playlist was a great way to introduce it to them. It was also a way to be playful and creative. One of my first classes was on what was one of the coldest days of the year. As students entered the class, I was blasting the Fresh Prince and DJ Jazzy Jeff's "Summertime." "You've got to be kidding GLB!" one of the students declared. "No, just think about the song," I replied. By the end of the track we were grooving and I was explaining some of the specific Philadelphia references (e.g., "the plateau" and "sneaks"). It was still ridiculously cold in Madison, Wisconsin but for about 4 minutes we were experiencing "summertime!"

Elements of hip hop pedagogical flows. In his brilliant short film, *Hip Hop Genius: Remixing High School Education*, Sam Seidel (2011) describes elements of Hip Hop that are useful for classroom teachers who want to engage and be successful with 21st century learners. These elements include: flipping something out of nothing, staying fresh, sampling and mixing, and employing creative resourcefulness.

Flipping something out of nothing. Most poor people understand this principle. Many of my elementary school classmates and I had times when our families ran out of aluminum foil or plastic wrap. On those days, we brought our sandwiches wrapped in the plastic bag the loaf of bread came in. Our mamas flipped something out of nothing. Or perhaps our dad's car was missing an antennae and he substituted a coat hanger. He was flipping something out of nothing. Teachers who flip something out of nothing are not dissuaded by a lack of supplies or materials. When I decided to teach *Romeo and Juliet* to my middle school students, I kept hearing how it was a "high school book" and I should not be teaching it to 13-year-olds. To introduce the book, I asked students a simple question, "How many of you have an older brother or sister who has a boyfriend or girlfriend your parents don't like?" That question generated lots of discussion and information about elaborate schemes that

90

siblings pulled off to see their forbidden loves. From there, I asked students to bring in examples of popular music about forbidden love. We listened to the songs and analyzed the lyrics. I also brought in copies of some of my own adolescent love songs (that caused a fair amount of laughter). Next, I had the students view the film version of the musical, *West Side Story*. Most of my students had never seen a musical before and we had fun discussing why the songs came in at certain times (e.g., when Tony lay dying and Maria starts singing, my students yelled, "Stop singing and call an ambulance!"). I did not have a teaching guide for teaching Shakespeare to early adolescents. I had to flip something out of nothing.

Staying fresh. Youth and popular culture place a premium on "staying fresh" or being innovative—in language, fashion, art forms, etc. As soon as a dance, slang expression, or hairstyle reaches the wider culture, young people switch it up and come up with new forms of expression. Hip Hop artists of the 1990s were known for their Adidas and jogging suits. Today's artists are often more eclectic looking for their own unique styles. A generation of basketball players wore their hair braided due to the influence of Allen Iverson. Today, we see Mohawks, locs, and blonde tips.

For pedagogy to be effective, teachers must also work to stay fresh. Teaching things the same way year after year will not work when students are used to the energy and dynamism of popular culture. The genius of the Children's Television Network's *Sesame Street* was its ability to incorporate fast-paced music and images akin to commercial advertising to attract preschoolers. In my own university teaching, I recognized how visual and technologically savvy my students were, and I started incorporating many more images and technologies into my classes. Instead of just having a "reading list," I have a "reading and viewing" list that incorporates film. I create course hash tags so that students can tweet during lessons. These electronic conversations allow for wider participation and more student-led discussions.

Sampling and mixing. One of the challenges of teaching in the 21st century is that our students come to us with very different conceptions of plagiarism, intellectual property, and copyright. Some of my most gifted student artists have gone to poetry slams and spoken word events only to hear someone on stage reciting a piece they wrote. When I asked how that happened they replied, "Well, I uploaded the piece online and I guess they liked it and decided to spit it!" They live in a culture that is a mash up where pulling from other artists is a regular occurrence.

Most teachers have lifted lesson ideas from other teachers. However, if one is truly going to be Hip Hop they will need to pull ideas from beyond teaching and education. The work of Emdin (2007) in New York is an example of using Hip Hop as an analogue for science teaching and learning. Rather than telling students to get into a small group, Emdin talks to them about joining the cypher. Instead of scientific argumentation, he helps students see themselves in "science battles" (as in "rap battles"). By sampling and mixing from Hip Hop, the students begin to relate to doing science as creating their art. They write "bars" and "spit rhymes" with scientific knowledge and concepts. One of my final assignments for my Hip Hop class was the creation of a mix tape. Students were asked to choose a social challenge (e.g., poverty, drugs, injustice) and create a mix tape of songs that spoke to the particular challenge. Along with the mix tape, the students also produced an annotated discography that explained why they included each song. I incorporated sampling and mixing into my pedagogy.

Employing creative resourcefulness. Finally, in order to be Hip Hop, a teacher must be able to locate and incorporate resources from a variety of places. In my early teaching, I landed a position in the Germantown section of Philadelphia. During the early European settlement of the city, Germantown was considered outside of the Philadelphia city limits. A number of the colonial leaders built "summer homes" in Germantown. One of the Revolutionary War battles happened in Germantown. I learned that my students did not know that their neighborhood was historic and filled with landmarks. Despite not having money for field trips, I organized a series of walking trips for students to truly see sites that they walked past every day. They learned about Cliveden House, home of Benjamin Chew and site of the Battle of Germantown. In the house was a set of china that Martha Washington gifted to Mrs. Chew. We walked to the Concord School House and Upper Burying Ground established in 1692 where Blacks, Whites, Jews, Irish, and Catholics along with Revolutionary War soldiers were buried. We made our way to Johnson House that was one of the Underground Railroad stations (safehouses). These trips did not cost us any money. We took our lunches and often ate outdoors in lush Fairmount Park. We made use of the resources all around us.

Years later, I read Paul Skilton Sylvester's (1994) description of the economy he created in his North Philadelphia third grade classroom to help his students understand how the loss of almost 60,000 jobs in their community was the result of larger sociopolitical forces. Skilton Sylvester took his students to local businesses, such as beauty salons and barbecue joints, and invited those proprietors into his classroom. His students built their own classroom economy with jobs he provided (and paid at differential rates). Before long, a few of his students started their own "businesses" because jobs the teacher provided were sometimes terminated or outsourced. Skilton Sylvester was employing creative resourcefulness.

When I began researching culturally relevant pedagogy, I saw how the teacher I referred to as Gertrude Winston drew her poor and working-class parents into the classroom. Miss Winston, a 40-year teaching veteran, told her parents EVERYBODY can contribute to the classroom. She had one of her mothers do a baking demonstration in which the students learned to bake sweet potato pies. Winston used the pies as a basis for teaching fractions. The students who had struggled with ideas, such as 1/8 is smaller than 1/6, quickly learned the concept when the pies were cut. She used creative resourcefulness in her extremely poor school community.

CODA

In my work to prepare teachers and teacher educators, I have tried to share the outstanding pedagogical practice of teachers I have worked with across the country.

I deliberately look for a mix of teachers to demonstrate what I mean by "being Hip Hop." I am not merely thinking about Black and Latinx teachers who are well versed in Hip Hop (or White teachers who are well versed in Hip Hop for that matter). I look for teachers who demonstrate the elements of flipping something out of nothing, staying fresh, sampling and mixing, and employing creative resourcefulness. With the help of technology, I have been able to "invite" those teachers into my classroom to talk with my students via Skype.

Over the past couple of years, our guests have included Karega Bailey (elementary teacher, Oakland, CA), Matt Cone (social studies teacher, Chapel Hill, NC), Steven Kahl (English teacher, Mountain View, CA), Julie Landsman (retired teacher Minneapolis, MN), Josh Parker (Literacy teacher, Baltimore County, MD), Yetunde Reeves (Principal, Washington, DC), and Ryan Vernosh (elementary teacher, St. Paul, MN). Three of these teachers are White men. Two are Black men. One is a Black woman, and one is a White woman. They range in age from their 30s to their late 60s. I have had the pleasure of teaching three of them. One I have known since she was a child. Perhaps only one would describe themselves as "Hip Hop" but all understand the power of youth and popular culture to inspire students far too many others have given up on. They also understand that the work they do with young people goes well beyond beats, rhymes, and Beyoncé!

NOTE

[1]   Latinx is purposely used in lieu of Latino or Latina to promote gender equality and gender neutrality.

REFERENCES

Chang, J. (2006). *Can't stop won't stop: A history of the hip-hop generation.* New York, NY: Picador.

Charnas, D. (2011). *The big payback: The history of the business of hip hop.* New York, NY: New American Library.

Delpit, L. (2006). *Other people's children: Cultural conflict in the classroom* (2nd ed.). New York, NY: The New Press.

Emdin, C. (2007). Exploring the context of urban science classrooms: Part 2–the role of rituals in communal practice. *Cultural Studies of Science Education, 2*(2), 351–373.

Forman, M., & Neal, M. A. (Eds.). (2011). *That's the joint: The hip hop studies reader* (2nd ed.). New York, NY: Routledge.

Gee, J. P. (2014). *An introduction to discourse analysis* (4th ed.). New York, NY: Routledge.

Haberman, M. (2005). *Star teachers of children in poverty.* Houston, TX: Haberman Educational Foundation.

Hale-Benson, J. (1986). *Black children: Their roots, culture, and learning styles.* Baltimore, MD: Johns Hopkins University.

Jay-Z. (2011). *Decoded.* New York, NY: Spiegel & Grau.

King, J. E. (Ed.). (2005). *Black education: A transformative research and action agenda for the new century.* New York, NY: Routledge.

Ladson-Billings, G. (2009). *The dreamkeepers: Successful teachers of African American children.* San Francisco, CA: Jossey Bass.

Nasir, N. (2011). *Racialized identities: Race and achievement and African American youth.* Stanford, CA: Stanford University Press.

Rose, T. (2008). *The hip hop wars: What we talk about when we talk about hip hop—and why it matters.* New York, NY: Basic Civitas Books.

Seidel, S. (2011, May 11). *Hip hop genius: Remixing high school education* [Video file]. Retrieved from https://youtu.be/WLMdkGk5Ofo

Shakur, T. (2009). *The rose that grew from concrete.* New York, NY: MTV Books.

Skilton Sylvester, P. (1994). Elementary school curriculum and urban transformation. *Harvard Educational Review, 64,* 309–329.

Gloria Ladson-Billings
University of Wisconsin-Madison

PATRICIA WALSH COATES

8. SEXUALITY EDUCATION AND THE SCHOOL DISTRICT OF PHILADELPHIA

The Importance of Community

WARNING! Going on this ride could change your life forever; result in poverty, heartache, disease, and even DEATH.

– Part of Why kNOw? sixth grade abstinence-only curriculum in Tennessee (2007)

Don't have sex, because you will get pregnant and die! Don't have sex in the missionary position, don't have sex standing up, just don't do it, OK, promise?

– Coach Carr from the movie *Mean Girls* (2004)

I remember going to see the movie *Mean Girls* (Lorne & Waters) in 2004 and thinking the aforementioned quote was one of the funniest in the film. A witty commentary on the multitude of abstinence-only programs that permeated public education during the second Bush administration, the filmmakers offered audiences a parodied view of what was actually taking place in public schools across the nation. And while at the time, I was amused by the coach's threats to his students concerning premarital sex, the implication is anything but funny.

Despite a recent decrease in federal funding, abstinence-only education programs remain the most widely used curriculum in public education (Guttmacher Institute, 2016). Even more disturbing, in districts where sexuality education is offered, the information given to students is riddled with inaccuracies and disparaging language centered on gender and racial bias (Kay & Jackson, 2008). This chapter endeavors to look at the current state of sexuality education in one urban school district whose state requirements toward sex and HIV education are restrictive at best. After an examination of the development of sexuality education policy in the United States, I explore policy and practice in the School District of Philadelphia in Pennsylvania and the community initiatives taking place to aid the district in providing a more comprehensive approach to sexuality education. My hope is to shed light on the importance of community action in districts (using Philadelphia as an example) faced with restrictive curricular policies in respect to how the district teaches students about decision-making regarding sex.

G. Sirrakos & C. Emdin (Eds.), Between the World and the Urban Classroom, 95–106.

A BRIEF HISTORY OF FEDERAL SEXUALITY EDUCATION
POLICY IN THE UNITED STATES

In 1919, Margaret Sanger, the leading birth control and sexuality education advocate in the United States, applauded the federal government for recognizing the need to teach sexuality education in schools. Touting the government's decision to dispense a "series of pamphlets on sex matters and venereal disease" a victory, Sanger proclaimed a "new day" for the birth control movement (Sanger, 1919, p. 3). Citing a pamphlet distributed by the US Public Health Service that stated, "An examination of the curriculum shows that society has had an official censor deleting sex from all classroom work under the orders of a now out-worn prudery" (as cited in Sanger, 1919, p. 4), Sanger concluded that "sex left out of all subjects" (p. 4) weakened and falsified the education process. A similar pamphlet issued by the New York State Department of Health urged that it was time for society to "look the sex problem squarely in the face, devoid of mystery and so-called 'moral issues'" (as cited in Sanger, 1919, p. 4). Sanger was delighted that both state and federal governments were issuing pamphlets presenting the same information and called the decision a blow to the "masculine-minded Puritans who still believe that women can be kept pure through ignorance" (p. 3). Sanger heralded the day when "medieval legal monstrosities will follow others of their kind to the dustbin" (p. 4).

These actions, and the woman touting their merits, were not without controversy. Sanger is generally criticized by most of her biographers as a racist for adopting early 20th century eugenic principles. Nineteenth-century eugenicists believed that mothers were "natural" eugenicists who would desire to reduce births because of a bad heredity or social situation. In her early writing, Sanger emphasized the need for contraceptives to control segments of the population. In *The Pivot of Civilization* (Sanger, 1922), she argued that birth control was necessary to alleviate the pain of mothering to a sickly or feeble child. She stated,

> We [eugenicists] do not object to feeble mindedness simply because it leads to immorality and criminality; nor can we approve of it when it expresses itself in docility, submissiveness and obedience. We object because both are burdens and dangers to the intelligence of the community. (p. 91)

She concluded by stressing the importance of birth control education as a means to relieve society of its social ills, not as a tool to control the lower classes. Yet many of her critics seized upon these passages and branded her a racist and elitist bent on controlling the lower classes.

Sanger's position on the eugenics movement was complex. Sanger (1922) referred to herself as a eugenicist in *The Pivot of Civilization,* yet she separated herself from the movement in other writings. Sanger aligned herself with eugenicists in their belief that the "unfit" should be "weeded out," yet she disagreed with their philosophy of promoting fertility among the "fit." Further, Sanger supported other eugenicists who called for population control; however, her support is often taken out of context. The full quote from Sanger's (1920) *Woman and the New Race* reads,

> Birth control itself, often denounced as a violation of natural law, is nothing more or less than the facilitation of the process of weeding out the unfit, of preventing the birth of defectives or of those who will become defectives. (p. 229)

Within the passage, Sanger discusses the need for women to practice reproductive self-autonomy in order to space pregnancies to benefit the health of the mother and child. A quote referring to "Negroes still [breeding] carelessly" is also falsely attributed to Sanger and often taken out of context. The quote, found in the June 1932 edition of *The Birth Control Review*, was written by W. E. B. Du Bois when discussing the effects of birth control on the debate between quality-of-life vs. race-survival issues for African Americans of his day (Du Bois, 1932). It reads:

> The mass of ignorant Negroes still breed carelessly and disastrously, so that the increase among Negroes, even more than the increase among whites, is from that portion of the population least intelligent and fit, and least able to rear their children properly. (p. 166)

Sanger (1919) strongly believed that the eugenic idea of boosting the fertility of the healthy was wrong. She argued,

> Eugenicist[s] believe that a woman should bear as many healthy children as possible as a duty to the state. We hold that the world is already overpopulated. Eugenicists imply or insist that a woman's first duty is to the state; we contend that her duty to herself is her first duty to the state. (p. 11)

Hence, I contend that Sanger's arguments for sexuality education and birth control were not rooted in racism but were born out of a desire to better the lives of women of all races.

Over the next 30 years, the support for sexuality education in public schools grew. During Franklin D. Roosevelt's administration, the US Office of Education began to publish materials and train teachers to better teach hygiene and sex-related materials. With a redesign of progressive education in the 1950s, classes in human sexuality could be found in both high school and college classrooms. In 1964, the Sexuality Information and Education Council of the United States (SIECUS) was founded to combat the conservative social hygiene movement, which had been issuing a restrictive curriculum that was often racially biased (Tupper, 2013). In 1968, New York University became the first institution to develop a graduate program to train sexuality education teachers.

With a growing panic over the AIDS epidemic in the 1980s, a new focus on abstinence-only policy in the United States returned sexuality education to a retroactive status. In 1981, the United States Congress passed Title XX of the Public Health Service Act, better known as the Adolescent Family Life Act. The act called for funding sexuality education programs that promoted "chastity and self-discipline" and other prudish approaches toward sex (SIECUS, 2010b, para. 4). Fifteen years later, Congress attached a rider to a welfare bill that established a federal program to exclusively fund programs teaching abstinence-only curricula and distributed $50 million per year for 5 years to state governments. Over those 5 years, funding for abstinence-only programs increased nearly 300% (Haskins & Bevan, 1997). States were required to match federal funds, thus funding for abstinence-only education exceeded $1.5 billion since the program's inception in 1996. One federal guideline under this policy required teaching "that a mutually faithful monogamous relationship in the context of marriage is the expected standard of human sexual activity" (as cited in SIECUS, 2010a, para. 8). The program harkens back to turn of the century misguided Victorian values where women were viewed as void of sexual impulses and sex was deemed an unclean act. This legislation, steeped in the notion that sex is a mutually exclusive act between man and woman after marriage, paved the way for repressive sexuality education policies that dominated the first 10 years of the 21st century.

In 2005, the second Bush administration requested an unprecedented $273 million for abstinence-only education, solidifying the position that sexuality education would no longer be the focus in schools. In his 2004 State of the Union address, Bush proselytized that to encourage teenagers to make the "right choices" about sex, Americans must "be willing to confront the dangers young people face—even when they're difficult to talk about" (Bush, 2004, para. 59). Concerned about the 3 million American teenagers who contract sexually-transmitted diseases each year, and with no mention that the United States has the highest teenage pregnancy rate of any industrialized nation, Bush asked Congress to double the federal funding for abstinence-only programs "so schools can teach this fact of life: Abstinence for young people is the only certain way to avoid sexually-transmitted diseases (STDs)" (Bush, 2004, para. 59). His administration argued that "we are living in a time of great change" (Bush, 2004, para. 105) and "yet some things endure" (Bush, 2004, para. 124), referring to traditional moral values steeped in a fundamental Christian ethic. Most important, Bush asserted that these morally universal values "are instilled in us by fundamental institutions, such as families and schools and religious congregations" (Bush, 2004, para. 56). Thus, implicated in the Bush plan for abstinence-only education was the use of federal funds to finance faith-based initiatives in schools to avoid the discussion of safe sexual practices in classrooms. Under the White House Office of Faith-Based and Community Initiatives, two funding streams (Special Projects of Regional and National Significance [SPRANS] and Community-Based Abstinence Education [CBAE]) allowed for money to go to religious organizations for the sole purpose of promoting abstinence-only programs in public schools. The president requested $73 million for the SPRANS project in 2004. By Fiscal Year 2006, CBAE increased over 450% to a total of $113 million where it stayed for 2 more years (Department of Health and Human Services Administration for Children and Families, 2006).

One program, the Silver Ring Thing based in Pennsylvania, went nationwide in 2005 with its public high school program of promoting safe sex through abstinence. This program offers "a radical response to culture's casual view of love and relationships" (Silver Ring Thing, 2016, para. 1), and its students are taught a message hailing the virtues of abstaining from sex until marriage. At the end of the program, students are given an opportunity to make a commitment to remain abstinent until marriage, receiving a ring, and in some cases a bible, as testimony to their pledge. On their website, the group alleged that "recent studies have proven the effectiveness of this type of pledge to significantly delay first time sexual activity," yet cite no sources or statistics for this claim (as cited in Walsh Coates, 2008, pp. 226–227). The program was immediately challenged by the American Civil Liberties Union (ACLU) in court. On May 16, 2005, the ACLU and Jenner & Block LLP filed a lawsuit that challenged the federal government's use of tax dollars to fund the Silver Ring Thing, which the plaintiffs claim is a nationwide ministry program devoted to bringing "'unchurched' students to Jesus Christ" (ACLU, 2005, para. 1). Three days later, the group significantly altered their website in response to the lawsuit and removed all religious references from its program. On August 22, 2005, the federal government suspended the flow of taxpayer dollars funding the Silver Ring Thing (ACLU, 2005).

Backlash against abstinence-only programs was swift with critics consolidating in an effort to discredit the Bush agenda and prove that the abstinence message was ineffective. After evaluating 11 nationwide abstinence-only programs, the National Abortion Rights Action League (NARAL) concluded, "The programs had no lasting, positive effect on young people's sexual behavior" and that by "denying adolescents complete information and by censoring teachers," abstinence-only programs recklessly "endanger youth" (NARAL, 2016, p. 4). The Planned Parenthood Federation of America (PPFA) referred to the programs as "anti-sexuality" education. In opposition to abstinence-only groups, PPFA designed a comprehensive sexuality guide for parents and educators, which is still available through their website.

Two of the most vocal critics of abstinence-only education at the time were Representative Henry Waxman (D-CA) and members of the medical community. In 2004, Congressman Waxman released a report concerning the state of abstinence-only education in the United States. The report concluded that abstinence-only textbooks used by schools and faith-based groups were filled with misleading and inaccurate information relating to abortion, diseases, and contraceptive use. Furthermore, Waxman (2004) discovered that many abstinence-only curricula, such as the one found in the Silver Ring Thing, blur the line between religion and science. None of the curricula gave information on the appropriate use of birth control and often exaggerated the failure rate of condoms. Beyond exposing the erroneous information pertaining to birth control, the Waxman report charged that many of the abstinence-only curricula perpetuated sexist attitudes and gender stereotypes, undermining female achievement and alluding to girls as the weaker sex. Waxman (2004) concluded the report by stating,

> This report finds that over two-thirds of abstinence-only education programs funded by the largest federal abstinence initiative are using curricula with multiple scientific and medical inaccuracies. These curricula contain misinformation about condoms, abortion, and basic scientific facts. They also blur religion and science and present gender stereotypes as fact. (p. 22)

The strongest arguments against abstinence-only education came from the medical community. The American Medical Association (AMA) released a policy statement in December 2005 stating that the federal government should not give grants to community-based abstinence-only programs unless it has solid scientific evidence that the programs are working (Hauser, 2005). AMA President-Elect Dr. J. Edward Hill announced that the prestigious association could no longer support curriculum programs that were riddled with inaccuracies and failed to present evidence of solid results (Hauser, 2005). The American Psychological Association (APA) issued a referendum calling for a comprehensive sexuality education curriculum that includes the explicit teaching of contraceptive use. The report stated that educating "policy makers about research documenting the limitations of abstinence-only and abstinence until marriage programs" (APA, 2005, p. 4) will show that "comprehensive sexuality education programs that discuss the the appropriate use of condoms do not accelerate sexual debut and yet do decrease pregnancy rates" (p. 2). In addition, the APA (2005) concluded the following:

> Comprehensive sexuality education programs that provide information, encourage abstinence, promote condom use for those who are sexually active, encourage fewer sexual partners, educate about the importance of early identification and treatment of STDs, and teach sexual communication skills are effective with sexually experienced adolescents. (p. 2)

The APA report was also concerned with the steady rise in HIV infections among teenagers, arguing that abstinence-only programs as a means of preventing HIV were not effective in the long term.

As scientific and statistical evidence showing the ineffectiveness of abstinence-only programs grew and a new administration moved into the White House, sexuality education policy began to change. In 2010, the Obama administration and Congress eliminated funding for two-thirds of the abstinence-only-until-marriage programs, including the Community-Based Abstinence Education grant program started during the previous Bush administration. In addition, two new sexuality education initiatives, the Teen Pregnancy Prevention Initiative and the Personal Responsibility Education Program, received nearly $190 million to provide innovative approaches to prevent unintended teen pregnancy and STDs, including HIV. A year later, the Division of Adolescent and School Health (DASH) funded $40 million to state and local agencies to provide STD/HIV prevention programs. In 2015, these combined programs received $213.9 million in federal funds to promote sexuality education programs in public schools. And while President Obama has called for the elimination of abstinence-only programs, the Title V Abstinence-Only-Until-Marriage program received an additional $50 million (SIECUS, 2010a).

Regardless of federal policy, it is ultimately up to the states and individual school districts to decide sexuality education policy for their students. The next section of this chapter endeavors to break down the policy in one urban school district— the School District of Philadelphia in Pennsylvania—and explore the importance of community in regards to sexuality education access. My goal is to explore the policy set forth by the state and the individual school district, identify the challenges the district faced in regards to said policy, and highlight innovative solutions the community adopted in the face of restrictions and misguided information.

PENNSYLVANIA POLICY ON SEXUALITY EDUCATION

Pennsylvania lawmakers issued the policy of *abstinence-plus* in the early 1980s. Abstinence-plus refers to comprehensive interventions that "promote sexual abstinence as the best means of preventing HIV, but also encourage condom use and other safer-sex practices" (Underhill, Operario, & Montgomery, 2007, para. 1) in contrast to sexuality education which is "a lifelong process of acquiring information and forming attitudes, beliefs, and values. It encompasses sexual development, sexual and reproductive health, interpersonal relationships, affection, intimacy, body image, and gender roles." (SIECUS, 2016, para. 1). Schools in Pennsylvania are not required to teach sexuality education yet must teach kindergarten–12th grade STD/ HIV education. Further, schools must stress abstinence in such classes. Elementary school curriculum can omit information on the sexual nature of how diseases are transmitted, and students in all grades can opt out of instruction if parents find the curriculum objectionable based on religious or moral grounds. In 2014, Pennsylvania and local entities received a total of about $7.35 million in federal funding across six sexuality education programs. The state received almost $1.5 million in federal funds for Title V Abstinence Education Programs with individual districts dividing $101 million in Teen Pregnancy Prevention programs. Most significant, individual districts, including Philadelphia, divided $988,000 from the Personal Responsibility Education Program, a first time funding stream to promote comprehensive sexuality education in schools (SIECUS, 2015). The School District of Philadelphia has adopted a sexuality education policy in line with state policy.

SEXUALITY EDUCATION IN THE SCHOOL DISTRICT OF PHILADELPHIA

I chose to review sexuality education policies in the School District of Philadelphia because of the district's size, diversity, and history. Established in 1818, it is the eighth largest school district in the United States, with 218 schools within a 3 mile radius. The student population is one of the most diverse in the country, with an estimated 134,500 students, over half being Black/African American, 19% Hispanic/Latino(a), 13% Caucasian, 8% Asian, and 8% multiracial/other (School District of Philadelphia, 2016). With a history of prolonged teacher strikes and state takeovers, the district has had its share of challenges. Included among these challenges is a failed sexuality education program, which has directly affected Philadelphia's students and their communities at large.

There are strong indicators that the abstinence plus policy currently in place is ineffective. According to 2013 Centers for Disease Control statistics, Philadelphia ranks fourth in a list of cities with the highest STD rates and has a teen pregnancy rate of 80 per 1,000 families. This rate is almost twice the pregnancy rate overall in Pennsylvania at 49 per 1,000 families (Kost & Henshaw, 2014). In addition, policy across the district varies according to need, with schools who have students with a higher rate of STDs identified and given additional instruction in STD prevention, contraceptive use, and sexual orientation. After a review of district curriculum and practice, it appears that policy varies not only from school to school but classroom to classroom (Baker, 2015).

COMMUNITY-BASED PROGRAMS OFFERING ALTERNATIVES

Community members in Philadelphia recognized a need for schools to provide a more inclusive approach to sexuality education that was apparently lacking in the curriculum. Two innovative programs in the city are aimed at bolstering the curriculum for students in Philadelphia. The first comes from the Philadelphia Department of Public Health (PDPH). The PDPH formed a partnership with the school district, offering lecture style assemblies on STD education and free, confidential STD testing in all of the city's high schools. The notoriously cash-strapped district was one of the first urban districts to partner with city health officials to provide additional services to students. In addition to lectures and testing, the PDPH works with community-based organizations, such as the Youth Outreach Adolescent Community Awareness Program (YO-ACAP) and Blacks Educating Blacks About Sexual Health Issues (BEBASHI), to identify at-risk populations for STDs. The PDPH (2016) has also partnered with Take Control (2016) to provide adolescents with information regarding the causes of STDs as well as testing and treatment options. The organization also provides free male and female condoms to various community sites.

The school district has also partnered with the Philadelphia-based nonprofit organization Access Matters to provide comprehensive sexuality education. Formerly the Family Planning Council, Access Matters strives for "big picture thinking" with "real world results" (Access Matters, 2016, para. 1), working as "fearless advocates for sexual and reproductive health, galvanizing stakeholders and policymakers regionally and nationally to de-stigmatize sexual and reproductive health" (para. 4). Access Matters has provided more than 8,000 counseling sessions in Philadelphia's 13 high schools along with over 500 student referrals for health services at an Access

Matters network provider. In 2015, Access Matters joined with the organization Concern for Health Options: Information, Care and Education (CHOICE). Founded in 1972, CHOICE became the leading advocacy group in the Philadelphia area offering sexuality information and counseling services throughout the city. Comprehensive sexual health education advocates the teaching of abstinence as the best method for avoiding STDs/HIV and unintended pregnancy, yet it also teaches about condoms and contraception. What makes comprehensive sexual health education effective is that it addresses every aspect of sexuality health and reproduction, including sexual anatomy, communication skills, self-esteem, responsible decisionmaking, challenges of parenting, and adoption. CHOICE continues to offer comprehensive sexual health education in schools and training for individuals interested in volunteering as CHOICE educators in schools (CHOICE, 2016).

Hoping to reduce the stigma around sexual and reproductive health concerns, Access Matters has developed a free smartphone app called It Matters, which includes information on a range of topics, including contraceptive use and access, HIV/AIDS, and health center locations. The goal of the app is to allow "youth to tailor their online information seeking experience with assurance of its confidentiality, allowing them to follow up and seek out in-person health services at their own comfort level" (It Matters, n.d., para. 1). Users of this app can identify and access health services that are made available regardless of financial situation or health insurance status.

I Matter: Preventing Teen Pregnancy is a program affiliate of Access Matters. The program provides adolescents with information regarding the importance of correct contraceptive use. Further, the program aims to establish partnerships and engage existing community partners to improve the lives of youth and their families by giving them relevant information to lead healthy lives and prevent teen pregnancy (I Matter Philly: Preventing Teen Pregnancy, 2015). Their website provides a plethora of information for teens and their families, including access to health care clinics, school events, and volunteer opportunities. Most important, it provides links to over 25 local organizations invested in providing Philadelphia teens with access to information to help them make informed choices regarding sex. Organizers of the program believe in the promise and importance of community action to their mission. They encourage other communities to follow their lead and get involved by supporting teen pregnancy prevention programs in their neighborhoods; providing safe places for youth to talk; volunteering with youth in the community; and promoting healthy life choices, including contraceptive use.

Two other community-based programs focus on providing information and STD testing for Philadelphia's at-risk youth. One program, iknowUshould2, is serviced through the Children's Hospital of Philadelphia and provides information on STDs along with free and confidential STD testing at multiple sites throughout the city (iKNOWUSHOULD2, 2016). The program relies greatly on social media to spread the message about STD prevention with support from trained health workers. Facebook, Instagram, Twitter, and YouTube all have iKNOWUSHOULD2 channels to provide youth with digital access to information. Similar in message, the Youth Health Empowerment Project (Y-HEP) has been providing HIV/STD information to Philadelphia youth since 1994 (Y-HEP, 2016). Y-HEP (2016) has a variety of community programs aimed at providing the following:

A trauma-informed and holistic approach to providing youth in need with the basic necessities as they transition into adulthood … with programs including peer-based outreach, youth leadership and political education, and a non-judgmental drop-in center offering harm reduction counseling and groups, prevention services, and therapy. (para. 1–2)

CONCLUSION

Twenty-first century sexuality education politics in the United States have been erratic at best, yet recent events have brought a shift in policy and ideology. In President Obama's 2017 budget, he proposed to eliminate the $10 million-a-year grant program for abstinence-only education run by the Department of Health and Human Services. Not only does this eradicate abstinence-only-until-marriage sexuality education funding, it also increases funds for the Teen Pregnancy Prevention Program and calls for a 5-year extension of the PREP (Office of Management and Budget, 2016). Furthermore, the budget proposal calls for an expansion of access to HIV prevention and treatment activities through the continued implementation of the updated National HIV/AIDS Strategy, which calls for an extension of community Personal Responsibility Education Programs and improved screening for Hepatitis C. However, it is the third initiative calling for prioritizing HIV/AIDS resources within high-burden communities and among high-risk groups that has the greatest potential to impact community programs in Philadelphia in a positive way (Office of Management and Budget, 2016). The success of this shift toward comprehensive sexuality education remains firmly in the hands of the community advocates who work with school districts. The National Coalition to Support Sexuality Education (NCSSE) includes over 140 national organizations who remain "committed to medically accurate, age-appropriate comprehensive sexuality education for all children and youth in the United States" (NCSSE, 2016, para. 1). The coalition, convened by SIECUS, provides multiple curricula and resources to community organizations and schools in an effort to provide comprehensive information for making sexual and reproductive health decisions. Organizations like Access Matters, CHOICE, and Y-HEP remain a crucial component to the success of community partnerships with schools to overturn antiquated abstinence-only curriculum and provide in-depth sexuality education to America's youth.

As I watched Hillary Clinton take the stage in Philadelphia on July 28, 2016 and accept the Democratic nomination for president, I couldn't help but think of Margaret Sanger. When Clinton asked Americans to join her if you believe we should "protect a woman's right to make her own health care decisions" (Bump, 2016, para. 93), I was in awe of the power of the moment and the progress made over the past century in regards to reproductive health. In a 1916 article written by Sanger for the *San Francisco Call and Post*, she boldly claimed that "great industrial changes which have taken place within the last half century have brought with them a great and urgent need for sex education" (Sanger, 1916, p. 1). Her statement in 1916 still holds true for 2016. As a historian of Sanger, I often wonder what she would think of current trends regarding sexuality education. I cannot help to think that Sanger would be pleased.

REFERENCES

Access Matters. (2016). *About us*. Retrieved from http://accessmatters.org/what-we-do/about-us/

American Civil Liberties Union. (2005). *ACLU applauds federal government's decision to suspend public funding of religion by nationwide abstinence-only-until-marriage program*. Retrieved from https://www.aclu.org/news/aclu-applauds-federal-governments-decision-suspend-public-funding-religion-nationwide

American Psychological Association. (2005). *Resolution in favor of empirically supported sex education and HIV prevention programs for adolescents*. Retrieved from https://www.apa.org/about/policy/sex-education.pdf

Baker, B. (2015, August 28). What a new app says about sex education in Philadelphia. *Philly Voice*. Retrieved from http://www.phillyvoice.com/sex-ed-flirts-technology-birth-new-sex-101-app/

Bump, P. (2016, July 28). Here is Hillary Clinton's presidential nomination acceptance speech. *The Washington Post*. Retrieved from https://www.washingtonpost.com/news/the-fix/wp/2016/07/28/here-is-hillary-clintons-presidential-nomination-acceptance-speech/?utm_term=.a7ba77cdab75

Bush, G. W. (2004, January 20). 2004 State of the Union address. *The Washington Post*. Retrieved from http://www.washingtonpost.com/wp-srv/politics/transcripts/bushtext_012004.html

Centers for Disease Control. (2013). *Sexually transmitted disease surveillance 2013*. Retrieved from https://www.cdc.gov/std/stats13/surv2013-print.pdf

Concern for Health Options: Information, Care, and Education. (2016). *Concern for health options: Information, care, and education*. Retrieved from http://www.choice-philadelphia.org/wp/

Department of Health and Human Services Administration for Children and Families. (2006). *Community-based abstinence education program*. Retrieved from https://www.acf.hhs.gov/sites/default/files/olab/sec2d_cfsp_2006cj.pdf

Du Bois, W. E. B. (1932). Black folks and birth control. *The Birth Control Review, 16*(6), 166–167.

Guttmacher Institute. (2016). *Teen's reports of formal sexual health education: April 2016 fact sheet*. Retrieved from https://www.guttmacher.org/fact-sheet/facts-american-teens-sources-information-about-sex

Haskins, R., & Bevan, C. S. (1997). Abstinence education under welfare reform. *Children and Youth Services Review, 19*(5/6), 465–484.

Hauser, D. (2005). Teens deserve more than abstinence-only education. *Ethics Journal of the American Medical Association, 7*(10). Retrieved from http://journalofethics.ama-assn.org/2005/10/pdf/oped2-0510.pdf

iKNOWUSHOULD2. (2016). *iKNOWUSHOULD2*. Retrieved from http://iknowushould2.com/

I Matter Philly: Preventing Teen Pregnancy. (2015). *I matter*. Retrieved from http://www.imatterphilly.org

It Matters. (n.d.). *It matters*. Retrieved from http://www.itmatters.me/

Kay, J., & Jackson, A. (2008). *Sex, lies and stereotypes: How abstinence-only programs harm women and girls*. New York, NY: Legal Momentum.

Kost, K., & Henshaw, S. (2014). *U.S. teenage pregnancies, births and abortions, 2010: National and state trends by age, race and ethnicity*. Retrieved from https://www.guttmacher.org/sites/default/files/report_pdf/ustptrends10.pdf

Lorne, M. (Producer), & Waters, M. (Director). (2004). *Mean girls* [Motion picture]. United States: M. G. Films and Broadway Video Films.

National Abortion Rights Action League. (2016). *Abstinence-only programs: Ideology over science.* Retrieved from http://www.prochoiceamerica.org/media/fact-sheets/sex-education-abstinence-only-programs.pdf

National Coalition to Support Sexuality Education. (2016). *A coalition convened by the Sexuality Information and Education Council of the United States.* Retrieved from http://www.ncsse.org/index.cfm.

Office of Management and Budget. (2016). *Budget of the United States government, fiscal year 2017.* Retrieved from https://www.whitehouse.gov/sites/default/files/omb/budget/fy2017/assets/budget.pdf

Philadelphia Department of Public Health. (2016). *STD control program, division of disease control.* Retrieved from http://www.phila.gov/health/diseasecontrol/STDControl.html

Sanger, M. (1916, June 10). *Tell girls things they should know: Mrs. Sanger.* Retrieved from https://www.nyu.edu/projects/sanger/webedition/app/documents/show.php?sangerDoc=320267.xml

Sanger, M. (1919). A victory, a new year and a new day. *The Birth Control Review, 3*(1), 3–4.

Sanger, M. (1920). *Women and the new race.* New York, NY: Brentanos.

Sanger, M. (1922). *The pivot of civilization.* New York, NY: Brentanos.

School District of Philadelphia. (2016). *Enrollment and demographics.* Retrieved from http://webgui.phila.k12.pa.us/offices/d/district-performance/repository-of-data

Sexuality Information and Education Council of the United States. (2010a). *A brief history of federal abstinence-only-until-marriage funding.* Retrieved from http://www.siecus.org/index.cfm?fuseaction=Page.ViewPage&PageID=1158

Sexuality Information and Education Council of the United States. (2010b). *A history of federal funding for abstinence-only-until-marriage programs.* Retrieved from http://www.siecus.org/index.cfm?fuseaction=page.viewpage&pageid=1340&nodeid=1

Sexuality Information and Education Council of the United States. (2015). *Pennsylvania state profile FY 2014.* Retrieved from http://www.siecus.org/index.cfm?fuseaction=Document.showDocumentById&sortby=Author&topicOnly=&topicRadio=&topic=&subTopic=&docTitle=&docAuthor=&publishState=&docDescription=&docPublishYear=&presentationSite=&FilterDocumentType=&FilterKeyword=&parentid=16&documentId=541&nodeID=1

Sexuality Information and Education Council of the United States. (2016). *Sexuality information Q&A.* Retrieved from http://www.siecus.org/index.cfm?fuseaction=page.viewpage&pageid=521&grandparentID=477&parentID=514

Silver Ring Thing. (2016). *Silver ring thing.* Retrieved from https://www.silverringthing.com/

Take Control. (2016). *Take control.* Retrieved from http://takecontrolphilly.org/

Tupper, K. (2013). Sex, drugs and the honour roll: The perennial challenges of addressing moral purity issues in schools. *Critical Public Health, 24*(2), 115–131.

Underhill, K., Operario, D., & Montgomery, P. (2007). Systematic review of abstinence-plus HIV prevention programs in high-income countries. *PLoS Medicine, 4*(9):e275. Retrieved from https://www.ncbi.nlm.nih.gov/pmc/articles/PMC1976624/

Walsh Coates, P. (2008). *Margaret Sanger and the origin of the birth control movement, 1910–1930: The concept of women's sexual autonomy.* New York, NY: Mellen Press.

Waxman, H. (2004). *The content of federally funded abstinence-only education program. U.S. House of Representatives Committee on Government Reform—Minority Staff Special Investigations Division.* Retrieved from http://spot.colorado.edu/~tooley/HenryWaxman.pdf

Youth Health Empowerment Project. (2016). *Programs and services.* Retrieved from http://www.y-hep.org/programs-and-services/

Patricia Walsh Coates
Kutztown University of Pennsylvania

MARK WOLFMEYER

9. ECOCRITICAL URBAN EDUCATION

Responses to 21st Century Challenges

For those of us with critical worldviews, our attention is consistently called to the gross injustices witnessed across racial, class, and gender divides as well as the poor health of all life on this planet. However, conversations regarding social injustice seem to happen over here and discussions about environmental crises over there, with little connection between the two. This chapter aims to break this false dichotomy of talking about social injustice separately from conversations about the destruction of the earth. Instead, I take the ecocritical[1] position that these issues are deeply entangled and the result of Western industrial culture's application of a "logic of domination" (Warren, 1990). Borrowing from Lupinacci and Happel-Parkins (2015), I use the term ecocritical to signify a trend in education and curriculum studies projects that interrelates social and environmental issues; the term includes and is not limited to ecopedagogy (e.g. Kahn, 2010), EcoJustice Education (e.g. Bowers, 2001; Martusewicz, Edmundson, & Lupinacci, 2011), and posthumanist projects in education (e.g. Snaza, Appelbaum, Bayne, Carlson, Morris, Rotas, Sandlin, Wallin, & Weaver, 2014).

I assert clearly that, yes, ecological issues should be, and increasingly are, a part of the urban education conversation. I justify this need in three sections. First, I highlight recent reports by leading human rights organizations relating the quest for social justice to human ecology and planetary health. Second, I discuss the entanglement of natural ecosystems with city life, drawing on both historical and contemporary examples. Third, I review the philosophers articulating consistent underpinnings unique to Western industrial culture that encourage social injustice and environmental degradation. In the final section, I piece together a vision for ecocritical urban education by assembling literature from a variety of disciplines, from famed ecological writings like *The Sand County Almanac* to place-based education and examples of urban ecocritical teaching in Detroit.

BREAKING DOWN THE DIVIDE: NGOS THAT BRIDGE THE SOCIAL-ECOLOGICAL CRISIS

In this section, I underscore the need for ecocritical urban education by providing examples of leading nongovernmental organizations that address social and environmental crises as interrelated phenomena. Assume for a second that as urban educators we were to prioritize social justice issues over environmental issues.

G. Sirrakos & C. Emdin (Eds.), Between the World and the Urban Classroom, 107–121.
© *2017 Sense Publishers. All rights reserved.*

Leading world organizations in social justice issues, like Oxfam, are now addressing such issues as they relate to environmental issues. Thus, as urban educators for social justice, we might have something to learn about Oxfam's new approach to eradicating poverty. Similarly, some environmentally-minded organizations are addressing social aspects as they relate to the environment.

The history and present mission of Oxfam positions it clearly as a social justice organization. On their website, Oxfam America's vision is "a just world without poverty," and their mission is "to create lasting solutions to poverty, hunger, and social injustice" (Oxfam America, Inc., 2016, para. 1). Originally based in the UK, as of spring 2016 Oxfam International comprises 17 independent Oxfam organizations across Asia, Australia, Europe, and North America. Consistent actions for these organizations include delivering emergency relief and long-term programs to eradicate hunger and poverty. Oxfam UK recently published an original discussion paper that highlights the need to look at the ecological when addressing the social concerns of Oxfam's mission and vision. The paper, *A Safe and Just Space for Humanity* (Raworth, 2012), positions the eradication of hunger and achievement of prosperity for all within "the planet's limited natural resources" (p. 1).

To begin the argument, Raworth (2012) lists elements of a just "social foundation" (p. 4), including education, energy, food, gender equality, health, income, jobs, resilience, social equity, voice, and water. Essentially this list is a breakdown of the items that Oxfam targets specifically. As the author argues, surrounding these is the "safe and just space for humanity" (p. 7) required to provide such a vision of social justice. A list of environmental issues describes the environmental ceiling, or those limits on ecologies due to human activity. The list includes climate change, freshwater use, nitrogen and phosphorous cycles, ocean acidification, chemical pollution, atmospheric aerosol loading, ozone depletion, biodiversity loss, and land use change. Putting these together,

> Deep inequalities of income, gender, and power mean that millions of people are living below every dimension of the social foundation. Nearly 900m people face hunger; 1.4 billion live on less than $1.25 a day, and 2.7 billion have no access to clean cooking facilities. At the same time, the environmental ceiling has already been crossed for at least three of the nine dimensions: climate change, nitrogen use, and biodiversity loss. (Raworth, 2012, p. 5)

The crux of the argument presents the necessity for policies that address both the social and ecological in order to enact long-term, reproducible social justice. Oxfam's discussion paper provides several justifications for why the environment and social justice are not and cannot be either/or. For example, environmental naysayers might say, "The earth cannot sustain feeding more people. If we were to eradicate global poverty, this would contribute more to soil loss and deforestation." However, Raworth (2012) writes, "Providing the additional calories needed by the 13 percent of the world's population facing hunger would require just 1 percent of the current global food supply" (p. 6). Similarly, for energy she writes, "Bringing electricity to the 19 percent of the world's population that lack it could be achieved with less than a 1 percent increase in global carbon dioxide emissions" (p. 5). Achieving this requires policy advocacy that does not increase the burden on the earth but instead identifies the inefficiencies and wastefulness of the wealthiest 10% of the world's population. Raworth (2012) writes,

> Social justice demands that this double objective be achieved through far greater global equity in the use of natural resources, with the greatest reductions coming from the world's richest consumers. And it demands far greater efficiency in transforming natural resources to meet human needs. (p. 5)

The discussion paper provides three angles for Oxfam's work in sustainable social justice: (a) an integrated vision that recognizes the role of planetary health in social justice; (b) a reframing of economic theory, which typically views damage to the planet as an externality or something that should not be worried about; and (c) policy development that accounts for a variety of metrics, such as natural and social metrics (like tonnes of carbon emitted and number of people in poverty), rather than simply economic measures like gross domestic product.

Likewise, environmental scientists are working with social scientists to address 21st century problems as intermixed and dependent on one another. Many examples of such scientific processes come from the Stockholm Resilience Centre, housed at Stockholm University. Their international board is composed of social and natural scientists, economists, and anthropologists. For example, board member and Princeton University biologist Simon Levin studies ecological and evolutionary patterns at the microscopic level, but his work has recently turned to the parallels between ecological systems and socioeconomic systems (Levin, 2000). Thus, the Stockholm Resilience Centre comprises a broad range of disciplines, and these scientists integrate their work for the cause of researching social-ecological spaces for long-term sustainability.

Research themes from the Stockholm Resilience Centre include global dynamics, stewardship, and urban social-ecological systems. In discussing their work on urban systems, the scientists at the Stockholm Resilience Centre describes the problems and possible solutions as follows:

> Urbanization patterns and the lifestyles of urban dwellers also affect the planet on wider scales in time and space. They contribute to shape bio-physical processes on planetary scales, and affect how humans around the world mentally connect with the biosphere. However, through their local to global linkages, cities can play a key role in the quest to continuously and increasingly support sustainable development. Our research aims to be part of creating a better understanding of the challenges that cities are facing, and importantly, to also be part of creating solutions. (Stockholm Resilience Centre, 2015, para. 1)

One example of research within this line is the Centre supported doctoral thesis of Joshua Lewis. Ultimately, Lewis (2015) analyzed the social-ecological resilience post-Katrina in New Orleans. His work proposes that environmental resilience, in some cases bolstered by government support, was concentrated within the White and wealthier neighborhoods of New Orleans. The poorer, largely African American, neighborhoods did not receive such support in redeveloping their environmental neighborhoods.

> Certain neighborhoods, (like the Ninth Ward) on the eastern flank of the city have experienced severe vegetation trauma, high rates of land abandonment, the expansion of emergent vegetation patches dominated by invasive trees and shrubs, and much more fragmented and uncoordinated landscape maintenance compared to more affluent neighborhoods. (Lewis, n.d., para. 8)

In other words, the efforts to sustain New Orleans were not equally distributed, and this research shows the inextricable link between environmental aesthetics and economic equality. Lewis calls specifically for urban policies that promote greater environmental justice that in turn will affect "oppressive social structures" (Lewis, n.d., para. 17).

Thus with a look at the current work of Oxfam, a longstanding social justice organization, and the environmental work of the Stockholm Resilience Centre, we see how the problems of social justice and sustainability are now beginning to be addressed in connection with one another. Although many organizations and efforts still treat these in isolation, some have indeed begun to recognize the interconnectedness of the issues and, therefore, the necessity to put interventions into conversation with both the potential to eradicate social injustice and bolster planetary health. Taking a step back to social and environmental catastrophes themselves, the next section provides concrete examples of urban ecological issues that further justify that we look at these issues in combination rather than separately.

STORIES OLD AND NEW: FROM CHICAGO'S MEAT INDUSTRY TO FLINT RIVER POLLUTION

Here I further justify the interplay of urban social issues with their ecological connections by highlighting specific examples, both from history and the present day. Environmental historian William Cronon (1991) provides several examples of these in his *Nature's Metropolis*, of which I will focus on Chicago's meat industry: its social and ecological effects. Looking at such histories begs us to make connections to the modern day, in which we will explore the recent Flint, Michigan water crisis.

Cronon's (1991) work offers detailed and complex histories of Chicago's development with a focus on its environmental history. He contends that Chicago shaped the landscape of the Midwest just as much as the landscape shaped the economics and politics of Chicago.

> During the second half of the nineteenth century, the American landscape was transformed in ways that anticipated many of the environmental problems we face today: large-scale deforestation, threats of species extinction, unsustainable

exploitation of natural resources, widespread destruction of habitat. It was during this period as well that much of the world we Americans now inhabit was created: the great cities that house so many of us, the remarkably fertile farmlands that feed us, the transportation linkages that tie our nation together, the market institutions that help define our relationships to each other and to the natural world that is our larger home. The nineteenth century saw the creation of an integrated economy in the United States, an economy that bound city and country into a powerful national and international market that forever altered human relationships to the American land. (pp. xiii–xiv)

As Cronon describes, as we attempt to characterize human geography in the US, we often parse out the city, the suburbs, and the country. On the contrary, Cronon's work targets this notion head on by confronting the symbiosis between city and country. As I will highlight, his work attends to both the social and environmental injustices resulting from these efforts.

Nature's Metropolis contains a chapter titled "Annihilating Space: Meat" that outlines the far reaches of Chicago's meatpacking industry. Primarily, it details how the market economies of Chicago evolved into food production having substantial impact on the Western and Midwestern landscapes. This takes place under the general principle that market logics view the natural world as a resource for exploitation. That is, profit can be earned by somehow modifying a natural resource with human actions. As Cronon (1991) suggests, the first example of this situated in Chicago and the great west, and related to animals becoming meat, is the massacre of the buffalo.

> The bison once had few predators. As a herding animal, it instinctively responded to attack either by standing its ground or stampeding. Both behaviors proved lethal in the face of market hunters carrying guns. Professional marksmen could generally take down an animal with a single bullet. If shot from a great enough distance, a bison could drop to the ground without arousing more than the curiosity of its companions, who became in turn the next potential victims .... Such shooting was hardly hunting at all; it was almost literally like working in a slaughterhouse, and the plains soon gained the appearance of a vast, nightmarish abattoir. (p. 217)

With the process well-defined, the natural resource called bison disappeared with great speed, all but vanishing by 1883. The hunters went bankrupt, and the owners of capital turned to other methods for market meat production.

Moving next to the evolution of cattle-becoming-meat, Cronon (1991) begins with the drovers who moved Texas longhorn up north. "In part, cattle produced many of the same grazing effects as bison" (p. 220); however, cattle moved within the boundaries set for them by the ranchers. The quest for greater exploitation of this resource led to the buying up of property for herding and driving cattle. Such consistent grazing had permanent effects on the vegetation landscape of the great west, including the proliferation of invasive species, and resulted in the increased use of fencing to control animal movement more fully.

An essential feature of the growing cattle-becoming-meat industry was the expansion and increased use of the railroad. The industry realized that driving cattle long distances to their death was not profitable because by leaning down the animals this travel led to a reduction in market weight. Thus, cattle were picked up earlier on their travels by train in places like Abilene, Kansas and then transported to the slaughterhouses in Chicago. At this point in time, the animal-becoming-meat process necessitated that the slaughterhouse and meat-packing stages be in close proximity to one another because decay immediately follows death without any human intervention of course. Resolving this issue was the increased use of refrigeration, first ice shipped from the north and ultimately the use of mechanically refrigerated train cars. Simultaneous to these developments were other new-found efficiencies in the animals-becoming-meat industry, such as a reduction in the input costs of feeding and growing the cattle. The natural diet of cattle (grasses) was expensive to maintain and led to using corn and the feedlot to fatten cattle. All of these changes, from the railroad to the use of land, were necessitated by the quest for greater profits in this industry.

Chicago, where some slaughter and most of the meatpacking occurred, endured its own ecological effects. These had specific social consequences, particularly endangering the public health with foul water and unsafe food. It is not surprising that the level of scale of meat production in this time period led to pollution of Chicago's waterways. However, the owners of the means of production did not see this problem as a public health issue as much as a problem of efficiency:

> Waste, then, was one of the symbolic paradoxes of meat-packing in Chicago. For those like Upton Sinclair who saw in the city all that was most evil in capitalism, Packingtown represented the decline of corporate morality and the end of an earlier, more familiar and trustworthy way of life. The stench in the Chicago River and the insidiously invisible substances that might make their way into a package of bologna appeared to be the product of companies so intent on their own profits that they were indifferent to the harm they did the public. Obsessed with turning waste into profit whatever the noneconomic cost, they sold what they should have thrown away—and yet did little to prevent pollution from the wastes that finally washed down their sewers. (Cronon, 1991, p. 253)

As I have reviewed, Cronon's work details the Chicago animal-becoming-meat industry as it impacted the social and environmental landscape of the city and great west. This is but one of his examples of such interplay between environment and city and, before moving to a contemporary example of this (specifically the Flint water crisis), I briefly discuss the relevance the animals-becoming-meat industry might have on urban education. This industry centers on the ethics and consequences of food production and consumption. Recent conversations in studies in education have discussed a related problem: schools teach students to be disconnected from food ethics. DeLeon (2011) wrote: "The ways in which we procure food for our society is a rich site of analysis and could be a point for opening larger discussions about the nature of oppression within the United States" (p. 184). In school, "students are given few choices outside factory-farmed food" (p. 195) implying an ideology of human supremacy over nonhuman animals and all species. Rowe (2011) describes that schools actively ignore the animals-becoming-meat process in support of industrial agriculture like that of Chicago discussed earlier. He recounts what it means to really know this process on a small-scale family farm against the absence of any such understanding of how a flesh and blood nonhuman animal has now become food on the school lunch plate. On the family farm, "what was obvious on the farm was the meaningful relationships and the sanctity of humans, nonhumans, and the land. Together, brimming with life, we literally fed off each other" (Rowe, 2011, p. 12), whereas with factory food,

> I participate in a monetary exchange where I buy a product with my money. I am not obliged to think about the farm, the origins of food, or about the once living and breathing creature or plant. All I see—and know—is right before me: an isolated object. (p. 13)

As an alternative, schools can teach about urban farming, thereby demonstrating that "alternatives exist to mass-grown and processed food, putting our sustenance back into the hands of the community" (DeLeon, 2011, p. 194).

Clearly, what is learned from Chicago's history is relevant to current urban education. I next move to a contemporary example of the interconnectedness of city and ecology: the Flint water crisis. Fortunately, several media projects today draw attention to the consequences of social irresponsibility and how these affect particular populations. At the time of my writing this, Flint, Michigan was drawing headlines for the high levels of lead in their drinking water. Many point the finger at politicians for their determination to save money and haste in making decisions. This is an important part of the story: an urban center with majority African American population and high percentage of households living under the poverty line requires our attention to such political maneuverings. We need to ask questions about power and representation in government and, thankfully, the neglect of many public officials led to their resignations. The people of Flint, however, must continue to suffer the consequences of lead in their water while measures are taken to both understand the problem and come up with a solution.

Citizen scientist Dr. Marc Edwards heads the Flint Water Study that aims to study the details of the situation and disseminate information to both keep the public safer and address the problem. For example, his group provided accurate and detailed information about the safety of using Flint water before it was switched back to a safer source. This included instructions for use in bathing and exact measures for drinking that included detailed instructions on how to flush the lines and use appropriate filtration (e.g., Edwards, 2015). This type of action is especially important for Edwards's efforts in promoting public health but for the purposes of this chapter, I want to dig deeper into his discussions of the cause of the Flint water crisis.

113

Most of the public understands two things: public officials did not take appropriate measures when switching the public water source from that of nearby Detroit (specifically the water from Lake Huron) to water from the Flint River and once the switch was made Flint residents had unsafe levels of lead in their drinking water. It would sound like the Flint River is polluted with lead, but this is not the case. The Flint River's water is highly corrosive to the supply pipes that deliver water to Flint businesses and residences. These supply pipes, a part of Flint's aging infrastructure, are made with lead. When Flint River water passes through these pipes, it corrodes the pipes which release lead into the water supply. So, the real question is: why is Flint River highly corrosive to lead pipes?

Edwards's research indicates that the highly corrosive element in Flint River that damages lead pipes is chloride. Chloride is a salt, and salt gets into the river at increasing rates when it is used on the roads during wintertime. When road salt is applied to melt snow on the roads, it initially stays on the road but over time melting snow and rain wash the salt away, carrying it into waterways like Flint River. In addition, the amount of salt used on the roads has been increasing. This is not the result of changing weather patterns (such as climate change) or an increase in safety needs. Using more road salt has come about simply because there are more roads in the area.

The uptick in road salt usage coincides with the suburban development of areas around Flint. This developmental process follows a pattern similar to the one evidenced in other cities across the United States. A 1978 research pamphlet put out by the Institute for Research on Poverty documented this phenomenon as it was happening.

> Over the past two decades, the plight of America's cities has become almost a commonplace of social comment. While city tax bases are eroding and their job markets declining as companies seek cheaper, newer, or more accessible facilities in the suburbs, their schools and services struggle against the combined impact of inflation, unemployment, and shrinking federal assistance. The cities are seen increasingly as deteriorating ghettos for the poor, unemployed, and the disadvantaged-above all, for minorities. In 1973, 64% of the metropolitan poor lived in the central cities. (Blakeslee, 1978, p. 1)

Specific to the Northeast, the pamphlet points out that nearby Detroit saw startling demographic shifts when, for example, it lost close to 40% of its college-educated population but only 16% of the population educated at or below eighth grade level (Blakeslee, 1978, p. 3).

Specific to Flint, Michigan, this time period of suburbanization has its own particular story. Between 1940 and 1960, General Motors (GM) opened eight new industrial complexes surrounding the Flint area in efforts to suburbanize or regionalize the manufacturing process. These efforts have been argued to not have an effect on employment opportunities for urban populations (Highsmith, 2014), but these analyses do not consider the segregation that takes place with such suburbanization and the subsequent effects on housing and schools, for example. Interestingly, GM proposed a regional government, a "new Flint," that might have counteracted some of these effects, but the political struggles ultimately resulted in little change to governmental structures (Highsmith, 2014, pp. 37–42). What is undeniable here is that suburban development in Flint, the result of GM's efforts to regionalize manufacturing, caused the increase in roads surrounding Flint, the increased use of road salt, the increase in chloride in Flint River and finally, together with irresponsible government officials with disinterest for Flint's urban population, lead in the drinking water.

My focus on the Flint water crisis is meant to be a timely example of the interplay between urban social processes and the surrounding environment. Deeper and broader analysis of such phenomena can be found, such as in the work of William Cronan introduced above. These stories are highlighted so as to underscore the need for teaching urban students human ecology. For example, students in Flint, Michigan deserve to know the details of their water crisis and how it came to be. This necessitates interdisciplinary understanding, including the science of pollution, the power of government and corporations, and the sociology of demographic shifts. The example illustrates that social justice conversations require a look at environmental justice as well.

LOGICS OF DOMINATION AS HABITS OF MIND

In this third section, I briefly review philosophers typically drawn upon in what might be termed an ecocritical tradition of educational studies. In other words, the discussion of the connections between social and environmental injustice have been theorized broadly and from many differing perspectives, with significant disagreements within the body of work. I do not intend to review these perspectives and distinctions but instead introduce some of the more relevant philosophical stances as they relate to the points made in this chapter. This intends to support the argument that, in addressing social injustice, urban education should address environmental injustice as well.

Karen Warren (2000) articulates a "logic of domination" by which Western industrial culture operates. This lumps together the "isms," not in order to make their oppressive natures equal but to demonstrate the consistency in Western thought, the omnipresent habit of mind embracing superiority and consequential power.

> To illustrate how differences are turned into justified domination by a logic of domination, let us suppose … that what is unique about humans is our conscious capacity to radically reshape our social environments to meet self-determined ends, as Murray Bookchin suggests. Then one could claim that humans are better equipped to radically reshape their environments in consciously self-determined ways than are rocks or plants—a value-

115

hierarchical way of speaking—without thereby sanctioning any domination or exploitation of the nonhuman environment. To justify such domination, one needs a logic of domination—a moral premise that specifies that the superiority of humans as Ups (here, their superior ability to radically alter their environment in consciously self-determined ways) justifies the domination of nonhuman natural others as Others, as Downs (here, rocks or plants that do not have this ability). (Warren, 2000, p. 49)

This logic of domination exists for the value-hierarchy of human supremacy over nature. Warren argues that similar logics of domination, acting almost as subconscious assumptions, exist in the case of White supremacy and male superiority, for example.

As some scholars of ecocritical education put it, such logic of domination needs to be "recognized, resisted and reconstituted" in schools (Lupinacci & Happel-Parkins, 2015, p. 45):

Social justice movements fighting against these injustices often have an arduous time creating and sustaining alliances among movements dedicated to eliminating human suffering and ecological devastation [and] we suggest there is an underlying common conceptual framework that perpetuates these cycles of violence. (p. 46)

In light of this framework, Lupinacci and Happel-Parkins discuss teacher preparation that addresses the logic of domination so that schools, in turn, resist and reconstitute the habits of mind that perpetuate violent actions.

Similarly, Martusewicz et al. (2011) term an ecojustice education as one that recognizes and reconstitutes the discourses of modernity, including individualism, mechanism, progress, rationalism/scientism, commodification, consumerism, anthropocentrism, androcentrism, and ethnocentrism. The final three explicitly refer to hierarchized dualisms, similar to what Warren termed the logic of domination, but the entire list reflects "the consequences of hierarchized and dualistic modes of thinking" (Martusewicz et al., 2011, p. 67). For example, mechanism is put forth as a habit of the modern, Western mind by which we think in terms of linear processes. "When we see systems operating step-by-step in chains of cause and effect we are using linear thinking" (Martusewicz et al., 2011, p. 69), and the consequences of such thinking include "a devaluation of living things from sacredness to physical objects and overlooking the complexity of living communities by reducing them to separate parts and cause and effect chains" (p. 70). Indeed, my earlier discussion of the Flint River water crisis is at once guilty of and a response to this habit of mind.

BRINGING SAND COUNTY TO CITY SCHOOLS

In this final section of the chapter, I call for work in urban schools that will address social and environmental crises. First, I pose the question of the relevance of teaching stalwart concepts in ecological movements with a specific look at Leopold's (2013) "land ethic." Second, I review urban education research responses to a related concept, place-based education. Finally, and in conclusion, I provide on-the-ground examples of urban education for 21st century challenges.

Since its first publication in 1949, Aldo Leopold's *Sand County Almanac* has sold over 2 million copies and been published in 12 languages. The work has had a significant impact on environmental and ecological movements across the globe, gaining fame almost equal to Henry David Thoreau's *Walden*. Within the book is Leopold's often cited concept of the "land ethic," which calls us to have an ethic of responsibility and mutual aid to the land as we would to each other:

> All ethics so far evolved rest upon a single premise: that the individual is a member of a community of interdependent parts. His [sic] instincts prompt him to compete for his place in that community, but his ethics prompt him also to co-operate (perhaps in order that there may be a place to compete for). The land ethic simply enlarges the boundaries of the community to include soils, waters, plants, and animals, or collectively: the land. (Leopold, 1949, p. 173)

Leopold (1949) calls to question the educational system, referring to a lack in its content regarding responsibility to the land. Typically, environmental education content teaches us to "obey the law, vote right, join some organizations, and practice what conversation is profitable to your own land" (p. 175). Leopold argues this kind of content steers us away from the following:

> An intense consciousness of the land. Your true modern is separated from the land by many middlemen, and by innumerable physical gadgets. He [sic] has no vital relation to it; to him it is the space between cities on which crops grow. (p. 187)

What relevance does this statement have for urban students and their teachers?

I do not suggest, and I do not think Leopold would either, that urban students or teachers have no relationship to their land. It is the educational system that discourages this relationship and thereby eradicates the possibility of a land ethic. To help, we can learn from science education researchers who focus on urban education. Some of this is situated within a sustainability science education that often focuses on place-based education. Lim and Calabrese Barton (2006) focus on the nurturing and extension of a sense of place in African American, lower-income, urban students. As Lim and Calabrese Barton (2006) describe it, place resonates with Leopold's land ethic, albeit integrating with the urban social system as well.

> A place does not simply mean a geographical location. We view *place* as a complicated, ecological system that includes physical, biological, social, cultural, and political factors with the history and psychological state of the person who shares the location. (p. 107)

Ultimately their contribution highlights how to draw out an urban student's sense of place that would encourage a more enhanced ecological relationship.

However, urban education students are not all the same. As Adams (2014) notes, studies like the above focus on students whose families have lived in a place for at least a few generations. What about families who have recently immigrated and have no knowledge of their current *place*? Her point highlights what might be problematic about bringing *Sand County* to public city schools. Having a relationship to the land is a somewhat bourgeois, romantic notion that entirely ignores political and economic realities for many people around the globe. In this way, the possibility of bringing *Sand County* to city schools is antithetical to the purpose of this chapter because it postures a land ethic for all that ignores several social injustices that dictate where and how people must live.

On the other hand, Adams (2014) proposes important considerations for how to foster place-based education for all urban students. She poses the following question: How can "immigrants and first generation people re/create a sense of place in an adopted environment?" (Adams, 2014, p. 341). To answer, she develops the concept of "multi-place" in her study of recently immigrated Caribbean immigrants.

> In [this] transnational community, ethnic-identified youth might construct their identity around a Caribbean place, whether they visited or not. Their notions of place and identity are largely based on stories from their parents and their lived experiences in the home and in an ethnic-identified community. (p. 351)

Many of these stories resonate with a land ethic, such as Adams's own recounting of her mother's "fluid connection between the indoor and outdoor spaces (p. 343)" in the Caribbean and her re-creation of this in Brooklyn.

Adams's concept of multi-place resonates with the land ethic of responsibility but does so in a way that does not necessitate knowing and staying in one place. This is an important consideration for teaching urban students and frees our efforts from the constraints of a political-economic naiveté. Knowing a place carries the notion that you have the freedom to stay in one place. However, we can draw on the best notions of the land ethic (responsibility to the land) with Adams's sense of multi-place to extend this to urban students. Quite the contrary to typical assumptions made about urban students, such an extension indicates (as it does in Adams, 2014) that urban students perhaps have a greater sense of place and caring for the land than their suburban counterparts.

CONCLUSION WITH EXAMPLES

This chapter was intended to motivate urban educators interested in social change by making an argument for the mobilization of urban educators toward seeing the interrelated nature of social justice and sustainability. This includes addressing all forms of domination and subordination, including anthropocentrism (human supremacy), because this habit of mind mirrors other hierarchies like White supremacy and male superiority. This is the philosophical argument posed in the last section. Earlier in the chapter, I described historical and modern-day examples of the interplay between urban systems and their surrounding ecology. These satisfied the philosophical underpinnings of the logic of domination in showing how environmental catastrophes are caused by such logic and in turn perpetuate social catastrophes and vice versa. At the chapter's beginning, I provided examples of nongovernmental organizations addressing 21st century challenges in total.

Coming full circle, this conclusion reviews two examples of urban educators putting these ideas into practice. More details of these examples can be found in Martusewicz et al. (2011) who call this work ecojustice education and situate it within ecofeminist philosophy. The examples are two Detroit charter schools, Hope of Detroit Academy and Nsoroma Institute, and Catherine Ferguson Academy for pregnant and parenting girls. Unfortunately, Nsoroma and Catherine Ferguson are now both closed for reasons unrelated to their good work in urban education that addresses social and environmental issues. It is my intention that their work will live on by discussing the curricular approaches.

The two charter schools integrated ecological crises and place-based education into their curricula. Hope of Detroit Academy's largely Latino/Latina students were led on a community inquiry project that began with a neighborhood walk to identify some of the issues present.

> The middle school social studies and science teachers planned an interdisciplinary project with the sixth-eighth graders to study the history and science of land-use in Southwest Detroit, especially focusing on the shift from agriculture to industrialization, the development of the auto industry, and the problem of brownfields in the community. (Martusewicz et al., 2011, p. 302)

The students learned several scientific methods of analysis as well as lessons in civics. The students and their teachers reported their efforts to local government officials and networked to plan and enact a neighborhood tire sweep, where illegally dumped tires in the neighborhood were collected and taken to be recycled into mud mats.

Nsoroma and Catherine Ferguson Academy intervened directly in the production of food. As suggested in the earlier section on Chicago's meat industry, the production of food is deeply embedded with social concerns. The Nsoroma Institute took head-on the concept of food deserts. This is the claim that urban populations are geographically isolated from healthy, fresh foods. In response, Nsoroma Institute teachers termed their work as food security and converted a city-owned park into an organic farm. They hoped to create "a template for other groups who might want to utilize some of the under-utilized land owned by the city of Detroit" (Martusewicz et al., 2011, p. 305). By including this in the curriculum, Nsoroma students would be learning about direct actions to take in response to social-ecological challenges. And by extending the urban educators' efforts, this lesson was also learned by the community.

Similar in their actions, Detroit public school Catherine Ferguson Academy featured,

> A fully functional farm complete with chickens, bees, rabbits, goats, two horses, a cow, all tended by the students. There is also a beautiful orchard of fruit trees, a large vegetable garden on grounds once used as athletic fields, and a barn constructed by young women. (Martusewicz et al., 2011, p. 306)

This school served Detroit's young mothers and young women who were pregnant, thereby addressing social matters head on. The alternatives to such a school are urban schools and school districts that inundate these young mothers with shame and blame (Luttrell, 2003). As far as curricular interventions, the school took on several environmental and social justice projects such as maintaining their farm for food security and renovating nearby buildings.

These examples motivate us to reimagine what our urban schools can look like. Reclaiming space for food security, student-led projects that target social and ecological problems in the community, and curriculum targeting commonly disregarded student populations all integrate the problems of the 21st century. Urban education can teach students through questioning and by example of the intersections of domination in Western industrial culture. By "recognizing, resisting and reconstituting" (Lupinacci & Happel-Parkins, 2015, p. 45) racism, urban education is required to address environmental injustice. In working to dismantle the logic that puts men before women, urban education can teach about the relationship among socioeconomic classes. Indeed, we must consider each of these intersections as fruitful places for exploring the interconnectedness of the urgent, pressing challenges we face today.

NOTE

[1] I borrow this term from my colleague and friend John Lupinacci who provided numerous suggestions and feedback for this chapter.

REFERENCES

Adams, J. (2014). Place and identity: Growing up bricoleur. In K. Tobin & A. Shady (Eds.), *Transforming urban education: Urban teachers and students working collaboratively* (pp. 341–354). Boston, MA: Sense Publishers.

Blakeslee, J. (1978). 'White flight' to the suburbs: A demographic approach. *Institute for Research on Poverty Newsletter, 3*(2), 1–4.

Bowers, C. A. (2001). *Educating for eco-justice and community.* Athens, GA: University of Georgia Press.

Cronon, W. (1991). *Nature's metropolis: Chicago and the great west.* New York, NY: Norton.

DeLeon, A. (2011). What's that non-human doing on your lunch tray: Disciplinary spaces, school cafeterias, and possibilities of resistance. In S. A. Robert & M. B. Weaver-Hightower (Eds.), *School food politics: The complex ecology of hunger and feeding in schools around the world* (pp. 183–200). New York, NY: Peter Lang.

Edwards, M. (2015). *Lead in drinking water: Health risks to Flint residents.* Retrieved from http://flintwaterstudy.org/2015/09/lead-in-drinking-water-health-risks-to-flint-residents/

Highsmith, A. R. (2014). Beyond corporate abandonment: General Motors and the politics of metropolitan capitalism in Flint, Michigan. *Journal of Urban History, 40*(1), 31–47.

Kahn, R. (2010). *Critical pedagogy, ecoliteracy and planetary crisis: The ecopedagogy movement.* New York, NY: Peter Lang.

Leopold, A. (1949). *A sand county almanac.* New York, NY: Oxford University Press.

Levin, S. (2000). *Fragile dominion: Complexity and the commons.* New York, NY: Basic Books.

Lewis, J. (2015). *Deltaic dilemmas: Ecologies of infrastructure in New Orleans* (Doctoral thesis, Stockholm Resilience Centre, Stockholm, Sweden). Retrieved from https://www.diva-portal.org/smash/get/diva2:845118/FULLTEXT01.pdf

Lewis, J. (n.d.). *The weeds are thicker on the poorer side of town.* Retrieved from http://www.stockholmresilience.org/research/research-news/2015-08-25-the-weeds-are-thicker-on-the-poorer-side-of-town.html

Lim, M., & Calabrese Barton, A. (2006). Science learning and a sense of place in a urban middle school. *Cultural Studies in Science Education, 1*(1), 107–142.

Lupinacci, J., & Happel-Parkins, A. (2015). Recognize, resist, and reconstitute: An ecocritical conceptual framework. *The SoJo Journal: Educational Foundations and Social Justice Education, 1*(1), 45–61.

Luttrell, W. (2003). *Pregnant bodies, fertile minds: Race, gender, and the schooling of pregnant teens.* New York, NY: Routledge.

Martusewicz, R., Edmundson, J., & Lupinacci, J. (2011). *Ecojustice education: Toward diverse, democratic, and sustainable communities.* New York, NY: Routledge.

Oxfam America, Inc. (2016). *Inside Oxfam America.* Retrieved from http://www.oxfamamerica.org/explore/inside-oxfam-america/

Raworth, K. (2012). *A safe and just space for humanity: Can we live within the doughnut?* Oxfam Discussion Paper. Retrieved from https://www.oxfam.org/sites/www.oxfam.org/files/dp-a-safe-and-just-space-for-humanity-130212-en.pdf

Rowe, B. (2011). Understanding animals-becoming-meat: Embracing a disturbing education. *Critical Education, 2*(7), 1–25.

Snaza, N., Appelbaum, P., Bayne, S., Carlson, D., Morris, M., Rotas, N., Sandlin, J., Wallin, J, & Weaver, J. (2014). Towards a posthumanist education. *Journal of Curriculum Theorizing, 30*(2), 39–55.

Stockholm Resilience Centre. (2015). *Urban social-ecological systems.* Retrieved from http://www.stockholmresilience.org/21/research/research-themes/urban.html

Warren, K. (1990). The power and promise of ecological feminism. *Environmental Ethics, 12,* 125–146.

Warren, K. (2000). *Ecofeminist philosophy: A Western perspective on what it is and why it matters.* New York, NY: Rowman and Littlefield.

Mark Wolfmeyer
Kutztown University of Pennsylvania

SHIRLEY R. STEINBERG

AFTERWORD

Onward Urban Soldiers

An afterword to a book about urban education can only be considered yet another foreword. As an unrecognized field of study by dominant culture, urban education is an American family secret. We all know it exists, or at least it should exist, but the grownups do not know what to do with it. Sisyphean attempts by urban educators to create a conversation between the government and teachers are deflected or blocked; publishers are selected to create standardized textbooks and tests. And urban education is ignored.

After Ronald Reagan's National Commission on Excellence in Education released *A Nation at Risk* in 1983, Americans were put on notice that students were not competitive in the global education market. Indeed, the commission noted that teachers were, in short, failing. Pulling up our educational bootstraps, we were told that the school year should be longer, testing and standards must be more rigorous, college entrance requirements were not stringent enough, and teachers should be evaluated with metrics reflected in good business practice. *A Nation at Risk* ushered in neo-liberal American education, articulating the goals to make students competitive. Urban education was not a topic, indeed, American education was re-articulated to be one size fits all…certainly no room for urban education. Fun fact: the Commission contained 18 members, one of whom was a school teacher.

We have never understood why our students need to be competitive with other nations, but we are reminded of this humiliation often. After almost four decades, few recommendations have been enacted, however American demagoguery from right-wing political unwashed masses has insisted that the failure of our students continues to rest in the lack of rote memorization, national curriculum, running records, and continual high stakes testing. Political promises, uninformed and naïve are delivered by the *wha wha* from a *Peanuts* cartoon strip. The inventory of American educational reforms is a *Saturday Night Live* skit gone bad: 1000 Points of Light, No Child Left Behind, Race to the Top, phrases spewed and promises unfulfilled…teachers are blamed, and students are failing. And what about urban students? In a one-size-fits-all mandate, there are no urban students.

For decades, scholars and teachers, parents and activists have attempted to influence governmental dictates on education, but then again, American educational decisions are made by the reigning political party, the basketball playing buddy

G. Sirrakos & C. Emdin (Eds.), Between the World and the Urban Classroom, 123–124.

Secretary of Education, or, as in post-2016 election America, the pyramid scheme queen of bleach and detergent…peppered with publishing companies' abilities to weasel themselves into state curriculum boards. Our voices have fallen on the deaf ears of those who refuse to hear. Urban schools are defunded, closed, re-invented, and then closed again. Urban students fail, not because they want to, but because school is not a place to thrive and learn, it is a containment facility stocked with books containing an irrelevant, insulting curriculum. Schools in urban America are set up to fail.

How does one integrate a critical curriculum in a nation that refuses to contextualize urban education? The ways of seeing discussed by the authors in this book are framed with a socio-theoretical lens which demands that power be recognized and called out. As critical pedagogy has reminded us these past years, power must be identified, and questions asked: *How does power work? Who benefits from educational decisions?* And as we have been reminded, we must create a pedagogical revolution from within, and in the confines of our own classes. This book represents grassroots ways of knowing which inform and usurp the mega-corporate sycophants at the podium. We refuse to allow urban education to be sidelined before it is even acknowledged; and, we name exactly what urban education is: educating those who those in power want to keep powerless.

This book insists we engage our urban students in creating authentic, culturally relevant, and critically pedagogical urban education. We are at war; there is no mistaking this. This is a war of context and a war for the future of our children and youth. We must fight against greed and exploitation, and that without stepping up and out, the war will be lost. In these desperate times, we must do more than stare into our *best practices* abyss and motivate those invested in our future to create an equitable, socially contextual urban education. We should consider this book as the foreword, the preface to calling out what is wrong in education, and demanding distinct and appropriate programs and funding for what can be right in education. We have read this book, now we act.

Shirley R. Steinberg
Research Professor of Critical Youth Studies
University of Calgary

ABOUT THE AUTHORS

Wayne Au is an Associate Professor in the School of Educational Studies at the University of Washington Bothell, and he is an editor for the social justice education magazine, *Rethinking Schools*. A former public high school teacher, Au's research focuses on critical education policy studies, curriculum theory, and teaching for social justice. He most recently coauthored the book, *Reclaiming the Multicultural Roots of U.S. Curriculum.*

Arash Daneshzadeh is a Lecturer in the School of Education, Department of Leadership Studies at the University of San Francisco. He is also editor of the *International Journal of Peace Studies*. Daneshzadeh is a refugee, former systems-impacted youth, and scholar-activist who has worked with incarcerated youth and adults for 15 years. The crux of his praxis focuses on forging a bridge between community engagement and school organizational behavior. His current scholarship aims to uproot the historical legacy of settler colonialism as it continues to metastasize within school discipline norms and youth interventions. He is coeditor and chapter contributor of the recent book, *Understanding, Dismantling, and Disrupting the Prison-To-School Pipeline.*

Christopher Emdin is an Associate Professor in the Department of Mathematics, Science and Technology at Teachers College, Columbia University. He serves as Director of Science Education at the Center for Health Equity and Urban Science Education and Associate Director of the Institute for Urban and Minority Education at Teachers College, Columbia University. Emdin serves as a Minorities in Energy Ambassador for the U.S. Department of Energy and the STEAM Ambassador for the U.S. Department of State. Emdin is a social critic whose commentary on issues of race, culture, and inequality in education have appeared in dozens of influential periodicals, including the *New York Times*, *Wall Street Journal*, and *Washington Post*. He is the author of the award winning books, *Urban Science Education for the Hip-hop Generation* and *For White Folks Who Teach in the Hood and the Rest of Y'all Too.*

Venus E. Evans-Winters is an Associate Professor of Education at Illinois State University in the Department of Educational Administration and Foundations and Faculty Affiliate in Women & Gender Studies and Ethnic Studies. Her teaching interests are educational policy studies, social foundations of education, and qualitative research methods. Evans-Winters's research areas are school resilience, critical urban education, and critical race theory and feminism(s). She is the author of *Teaching Black Girls: Resiliency in Urban Classrooms* and coeditor of *(Re)Teaching Trayvon: Education for Racial Justice and Human Freedom.*

Gloria Ladson-Billings is the Kellner Family Distinguished Chair of Urban Education in the Department of Curriculum & Instruction at the University of Wisconsin - Madison. Ladson-Billings is also a faculty affiliate in the Departments of Educational Policy Studies, Educational Leadership & Policy Analysis, and Afro American Studies. Ladson-Billings was the 2005–2006 President of the American Educational Research Association (AERA) and is the incoming (November 2017) President of the National Academy of Education.

Treva B. Lindsey is an Associate Professor of Women's, Gender, and Sexuality Studies at The Ohio State University. She is the inaugural Equity for Women and Girls of Color Fellow at Harvard University (2016-2017). She is also the recipient of several awards and fellowships. She is a guest contributor to traditional and digital forums such as *Al Jazeera*, *BET*, *Complex Magazine*, and *Cosmopolitan*.

George Sirrakos Jr. is an Assistant Professor in the Department of Secondary Education at Kutztown University of Pennsylvania where he teaches courses in education research, multicultural education, education foundations, education psychology, and methods of science instruction. His research interests include fostering equity in education, creating opportunities for students to inform the teaching and learning process, and cross-national studies of learning environments. Sirrakos was named a 2013–2014 Phi Delta Kappa Emerging Leader in Education for his work in helping advance the belief that traditionally marginalized students can also be successful in science.

Patricia Walsh Coates is an Associate Professor and Graduate Studies Coordinator in the Department of Secondary Education and Director of the EdD in Transformational Teaching and Learning at Kutztown University of Pennsylvania. She holds a PhD in History and specializes in both educational theory and 20th century feminist and trans-Atlantic history. Walsh Coates has joined a cadre of historians who examine the cross-Atlantic connection of ideas and policies related to birth control as a universal need for women. Walsh Coates has published various works in the field of teacher education, most recently on competency-based doctoral programs. She is the author of *Margaret Sanger and the Origin of the Birth Control Movement, 1910–1930: The Concept of Women's Sexual Autonomy*.

Mark Wolfmeyer taught mathematics in secondary public schools for 10 years on both the East and West coasts and is now an Assistant Professor of Secondary Education at Kutztown University of Pennsylvania. His research interests include educational policy, ecocritical foundations of education, and STEM education. He is the author of *Mathematics Education: A Critical Introduction, Math Education for America? Policy Networks, Big Business, and Pedagogy Wars*, and coauthor of *Philosophy of STEM Education: A Critical Investigation*.

Printed in the United States
By Bookmasters